In this, the second book of his Joy[...] of financial principles that he has gleaned from personal experience [...] reading.

Ryan takes the best of books such as Robert T. Kiyosaki's *Rich Dad, Poor Dad* and Fraser Smith's *The Smith Manoeuvre*, mixing it with wisdom found in George S. Clason's *The Richest Man in Babylon* (don't let the title scare you), and weaves in his own story of trial and success.

There may be some tools lacking in your toolkit right now, but Ryan will gladly lend you his! He is crazy passionate that you would live a life free from the burden of "have not" and possess the confidence to change your life and outlook.

I encourage you to borrow his tools, but more importantly grab some of his vision. You can go farther than you think and do better than you ever expected.

—Dr. Claude Page
Associate Pastor, Board President of ACM Ministries

My name is Shane Rau. I'm currently an independent contractor in the home renovation industry, and a worship leader in my community. In the past I tried many times to start a sustainable business but I could not gain momentum.

One Sunday morning in January 2019, a gentleman approached me and my wife to introduce himself.

"Good morning, my name is Ryan," he said. "I'm not exactly sure why, but God has highlighted you guys to me and I had to come over and introduce myself."

My wife Brandy and I made plans to meet Ryan and his wife, Megan. Over the course of a couple meetings, we soon discovered our mutual interest in business ownership and real estate investing. Ryan and Megan had experience in both of these areas while my wife and I wanted to learn more.

As we developed our friendship, Ryan suggested that I start a property renovation business. What ensued would prove to be an invaluable mentorship in the areas of business ownership and real estate investing. With his advice, I doubled my income in the first year and learned how to acquire consistent work from many clients.

Although I already knew how to do the work, I learned new perspectives from Ryan regarding how to run the business, manage my costs, and plan for the future. I now have the freedom to live the life of which I had been dreaming for a really long time. My business, and the level of joy in my family's life, has continued to grow as a result of the time and talents Ryan shared with us.

We are very thankful for what we have learned, and put into practice, from Ryan's teachings.

—**Shane Rau**
Independent Business Owner, New Moon Restoration

As a pastor, living with the knowledge that I would not have a pension, not having a lot of income to invest in RRSPs was troubling at best, and often a cause for sleepless nights at worst. Thankfully, after meeting Ryan and Megan and having some powerful conversations, we were introduced to a new and freeing financial mindset. They introduced us to the power of capital and the ability to invest in real estate to create passive income and open the door for a plan to retire. I never would have thought I would invest in real estate, but this journey has opened my eyes to a better future. They are both gems with a wealth of knowledge.

—**Jay Armaly**
Senior Pastor, Antioch Christian Ministries

THE JOYFUL SERIES

JOYFUL

You Were Made to Prosper

FINANCES

RYAN J. BONDY

JOYFUL FINANCES
Copyright © 2021 by Ryan J. Bondy

Printed in Canada

ISBN: 978-1-4866-2071-5
eBook ISBN: 978-1-4866-2072-2

Word Alive Press
119 De Baets Street Winnipeg, MB R2J 3R9
www.wordalivepress.ca

WORD ALIVE
—P R E S S—

FSC
MIX
Paper from
responsible sources
FSC® C103567
www.fsc.org

Cataloguing in Publication information can be obtained from Library and Archives Canada.

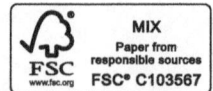

CONTENTS

Preface

For Christians and non-Christians alike, the word prosper has a wide range of meanings. In accordance with people's understanding of what's written in the Bible, I have heard it suggested that prosperity blocks one's entrance to heaven, while others have presented sound arguments based on the same Bible that God has called us to be prosperous in order to help build the Kingdom.

Regardless of your position, *Joyful Finances* is a book about joy. As the title suggests, it's about discovering joy within your finances, which is what I believe God truly intended for everyone.

As an entrepreneur for more than thirty years, I have enjoyed many aspects of business ownership and investing. What I've learned from life is that joy from money doesn't mean you have to have a ton of it. *Joyful Finances* is designed to expose you to opportunities that will increase the joy surrounding your current financial capacity.

Rich or otherwise, joy is really about having options. Throughout this book, I'm very much optimistic that you will discover many new options that will assist you in optimizing the joy in your life.

The Joyful Series

The reception to my previous book, *Joyful Wealth: How to Put More in Your Account*, was very telling. Society today is looking for a return of joy in their lives. All sorts of families—some of them dual occupation, others single-parent—have hectic schedules that include everything from parent-teacher meetings to activity commitments every night of the week, and twice on Saturday.

It's no wonder the world is crashing.

Having survived three decades of business ownership, real estate investing, and international commerce, the greatest joys my family and I have experienced haven't come from money alone. This came as a surprise to many who read my first book, but regardless of people's expectations their reviews and reception suggest that the book provided something they're very much in need of: joyful hope, encouragement, and inspiration.

In consideration of all this feedback, it seemed imperative that my wife Megan and I develop the Joyful Series, and what you're about to read is the second book. Additionally, you can find a daily dose of joy on our Facebook page (The Joyful Series). Visitors there will find a community built on a platform of cheerful support and optimistic assistance. You can also find out more about future titles in the Joyful Series.

The purpose of this volume, *Joyful Finances*, is to explore the possibilities of taking complete ownership over your financial affairs, to personally become the architect of your dream financial future. Yes, you will be encouraged to dust off that old dream machine, the one you perhaps forgot existed. Together, we will investigate money management tools, investment options, and even debt reduction strategies.

When you finish this book, if you come to be more excited about your financial position at the end of the month than you were at its beginning, we will have succeeded in our goal. Having created a family financial plan that allows us to look at the end of the month with excitement and enthusiasm, it is my wholehearted desire to assist you to do the same.

Read the pages carefully, being open to the idea that some of what you're about to read may seem unusual, uncommon, or possibly even impossible, but take notes and reread anything you may not understand at first glance. The ideas, concepts, and strategies buried in these pages have the power to transform your life in direct proportion to your willingness to embrace and employ them.

If you feel that your financial position today isn't very strong, we're going to change that starting now. As it is written, *"In everything I did, I showed you that by this kind of hard work we must help the weak, remembering the words the Lord Jesus himself said: "It is more blessed to give than to receive"* (Acts 20:35, NIV).

Introduction

The year is 2020 and it's springtime in Ontario. No sooner had we heard that the devastating forest fires burning up an enormous portion of Australia were finally under control than the news hit: a new coronavirus was spreading through China fast, and there was no cure.

When spring break hit in North America, travellers began returning home with the illness and it spread here as well. Suddenly, the world became captivated by a global pandemic. It seemed no corner was left untouched. People were dying, hospitals were overwhelmed, and governments around the globe ordered their economies to completely shut down until the headless monster could be contained.

It's been a couple of months since our collective introduction to COVID-19, and despite extreme precautions being taken by nearly every country, county, and even small town, the numbers have climbed to a staggering degree. At the time of this writing, tens of millions have been infected, a million lives have been lost, and fear and panic have swept the land.

In Canada, virtually the entire population was told to stay in their homes for weeks or months at a time, to only go out when it was absolutely essential. Thousands and thousands of businesses have been forced to close their doors, except for only the most essential of them. And even in those that remain open, like grocery stores, it's far from business as usual.

Before you think you may have purchased the wrong book, be assured that this is the perfect time to read about finding newfound joy in your life. It may be easy to argue that the world is falling apart, but where is the joy in that? The

Joyful Series has been designed to help you see that there is still an abundance of joy lurking in the seemingly dark waters we're surrounded by today.

God started preparing me and my wife Megan for this moment in late December 2016. Megan had been rushed to the hospital for an unexpected brain surgery, and she came home to recover in January with two new holes in her head. Waiting for her were me and our three diaper-wearing babies, all of whom had a new appreciation for this amazing woman in our lives—a mom, wife, business partner, and best friend.

But we weren't out of the woods just yet. Her doctors shared that there was a forty percent chance she would need another operation in six weeks. They would only know for sure once the first procedure had some time to heal.

Just two weeks after bringing Megan home, she was still restricted from driving, changing a diaper, or lifting more than five pounds at a time. At that point, we had to change more than twenty diapers per day!

Then we received another call from the doctor—and this time, it had nothing to do with Megan's brain. The news was about my spine.

"It's a miracle you're walking," the doctor said. "We need to operate on you right now."

When I went into the emergency room to discuss the situation with my doctor, he described the procedure. In it he would replace three vertebrae, drill into the core of my spine, and fuse a titanium plate to hold everything in place. You guessed it: this would be sure to lay me up with similar restrictions to those Megan was already under—potentially for months.

Fast-forward to mid-February and Megan found out she wouldn't require a second surgery. The doctors operated on me and I returned home in alarmingly quick order.

We were both healing, but the quake of these events rocked our financial world, altering the landscape of our corporate empire. Megan and I owned a local licensing bureau, a property management franchise, and an outdoor power equipment store and service facility. We also owned a property maintenance and building maintenance company, as well as an inflatable rental business. Additionally, we held rental and vacation real estate in both Canada and the United States.

And did I mention we had three babies as well? Right.

Before these medical crises, I had ignored all the signs, but we were overstretched, overleveraged, and our priorities were out of order. Megan had warned me we were due to crash, but I had an addiction to the thrill of business.

The adrenaline rush of adding new companies, clients, and contracts was like a high that a junky gets from a fix of cocaine. I was sick. God knew it, my wife knew it, and those closest to me knew it.

As you can likely imagine, when you take the top two people out of an organization like ours, things start to crumble. Within the time it took for Megan and me to recover from our operations, and me from my mental breakthrough, we closed or sold all but two of our businesses, sold a few buildings, and let go of our many employees and the responsibilities and stress related to managing them.

Through these circumstances, we discovered a new perspective. Despite our greatest financial challenges in years, we embraced joy in our family and home like never before. It felt like we were being led down a new path, and that it would be great regardless of how different the next portion of our journey was.

We knew God wanted to do something amazing in our lives, and He now had our full attention.

In the three years following our operations, Megan and I built our lives around two basic principles. First, before making major decisions, we asked God if this was something He wanted us to do, and then quietly waited for the answer. Second, we determined that every decision we made for our family would be predicated on whether the result of the decision would bring additional joy into our home.

In *Joyful Wealth*, you can read about the various areas in which we found incredible improvement by using these two principles as our guide.

As we moved forward, we became amazed at how much joy already existed in our home. An abundance of joy seemed to live in every corner, but we'd been so distracted for years that we'd failed to recognize it. Without experiencing the elusive happiness we had always dreamed of, we had chased it even harder.

Here's the thing: money is no laughing matter. When the bills are on the table and each dollar seems to need four brothers or sisters to help cover the debts, it's hard to find joy. Megan and I had to take a hard look at our financial position and realize that we had to make significant changes, now that we had only a fraction of the income we'd had before.

And so it began.

This book provides an outline of some of the decisions Megan and I have successfully implemented in order to live a more joyfully optimistic lifestyle. To be clear, we aren't rich and famous, and yet at the end of each month we are more excited about our financial future than we were at the beginning. That is what it means to have joyful finances.

Joyful Finances is designed to serve as a tool in the war on financial joy. Do not allow your financial position to steal one more moment of joy from your life. Now is the time to take a stand against the enemy, to protect your own army of soldiers and overcome the battlefields that may have held you captive in your life.

Megan and I are so grateful that God brought us through the last few years, guiding us safely to the other side. It's more important than ever today that we place our faith in Him.

Taking control of your life doesn't mean you have to fight the battle alone. The stage is set, you're holding a military strategy map, and now it's your move. Enjoy, and may your financial future include all the joy you ever dreamed possible!

PART

The Power to Look Ahead

ONE

1

"For I know the plans I have for you," says the Lord.
"They are plans for good and not for disaster,
to give you a future and a hope."
(Jeremiah 29:11, NLT)

You know you've seen it, that scene in a movie where a fortune-teller gazes into the depths of a crystal ball and makes claims about the future. Why a crystal ball? Is it really crystal? What if it were just plain old glass? Would it still work? What if it were cracked somehow?

In 2009, I was blessed with the gift of my very own crystal ball, given to me by an incredibly special friend. The owner of a decor store herself, Kathy came to visit me one day with a genuine concern for my wellbeing. She knew I was reeling from a divorce earlier that year, one that would set me back seven digits in debt, living alone in a big empty house and running a business that demanded more concentration than I was able to direct, with bills coming at me from every angle.

Kathy hadn't come to offer me a loan, or to pay my bills, but what she did give me was worth several times more than any of those things. She brought me hope in the form of a crystal ball—a shattered one, in fact. The glass was frosted and stress lines ran all over its surface. She placed it on a small tripod on the centre of my fireplace mantle.

I gazed at her with a look of slight confusion.

Kathy turned to me. "Ryan, you might think your future is cloudy and uncertain right now, but you're a winner. You always have been. You need to dream again, like you used to dream, and when you look into this crystal ball you will know that this cloudy season will soon pass. Your future is bright and full of endless possibilities, just like it always has been. If you can dream it, you can achieve it!"

I love that woman, and the gift she presented me that day was like no other. She assured me that I was still in control. Always have been, always will be.

Kathy's cloudy crystal ball reminded me that despite the storms in our lives, or the stresses that try to shatter our vision, we must continue to look to the future with confidence that everything is going to be better than we can imagine in the moment. In other words, even when the future is unclear, we need to continue to dream about it in such detail that we remain focused on what's important, on where we truly want to end up.

Proverbs 29:18 states, *"Where there is no vision, the people perish..."* (KJV). And this is where we're going to start, because from where I was that day, there was nowhere to go but up.

Now let's fast-track about a dozen years.

"I love to dream," I said to Megan as we walked down a gorgeous gravel road next to a lake. Large beachside houses rose around us, surrounded by pine trees that stretched nearly a hundred feet into the air. Ahead of us, the children hustled along.

I drifted off a moment as we enjoyed the evening walk as a family. I couldn't help but wonder what life would look like if we were in a position to own one of these cottages, for which the property taxes each year cost nearly the same as what we'd paid for our three-year-old minivan.

We passed house after house, property after property. I loved walking by them in wonder of how these people managed it. Boats lined the driveways, the lawns were well cared for, beautiful custom-formed metal roofs topped the cottages, and their huge bay windows provided panoramic views of the water and woods. And how could I forget those incredible wraparound porches that provided guests with a perfect resting place any time of day?

These cottages were people's second, or even third, homes... the places they visited for a week or two when the weather was right, just to enjoy a change of scenery. I loved them!

I may sound envious, but I assure you I am not. Because I've always been a gigantic dreamer, these opportunities to witness success are incredibly encouraging to me. They illustrate future possibilities. My thought has always been, *If someone else can do this, why can't I?*

This may seem like an unusual place to begin, but let me segue into a story about a young man from Pretoria, South Africa. This man was born in 1971, and by the time he was in his late twenties he was a multimillionaire with a stake to fame stemming from his entrepreneurial efforts to found X.com in 1999 (which later became PayPal), SpaceX in 2002, and Tesla Motors in 2003. You may have heard of him before. His name is Elon Musk.

Musk is no stranger on the world's business scene. One of his current aspirations is to colonize Mars. This guy is a dreamer of epic proportions. It could be said that he is a tremendous success because of his ability to dream, and not the other way around. In other words, he doesn't dream big because he is a success; he is a success because he dreamt of being one.

But what does dreaming have to do with your finances?

In his astonishing speech delivered on August 28, 1963, Martin Luther King Jr. inspired millions of Americans and began to transform the world with his powerful words "I have a dream." Now, more than half a century later, his speech and its vision to eliminate racism in America is still often replayed. From 1957 to 1968, King travelled more than six million miles and spoke about 2,500 times, each time sharing his message and changing the world. That was a powerful dream.

It may be reasoned that nearly every significant accomplishment in life began first with a dream—or a nightmare, in some cases. Dreams have been responsible for major creative and scientific discoveries throughout the course of human history. From sci-fi novels to inspirational music, from quantum mechanics to the speed of light, many creatives and inventors say that their inspiration began with a dream.[1]

In my previous book, *Joyful Wealth*, I also discussed the importance of dreaming. In fact, I decided to begin this book in a similar fashion, because only through allowing yourself to dream can you grant yourself permission to see things as you wish to see them, not necessarily as they are at this exact moment in time. For many, this is not easily done. For some, it may be downright nauseating. When was the last time you allowed yourself to dream? I mean *really* dream? When was the last time you closed your eyes and imagined a world exactly as you would like to see it?

---

[1] For more information on dreams that changed the course of human history, I encourage you to refer to the work of author Rebecca Turner, the founder of World of Lucid Dreaming. Her work has highlighted the likes of Albert Einstein and Paul McCartney, among others who have impacted the world as we know it through the realization of their dreams.

Elon Musk and Dr. Martin Luther King Jr. both had a tremendous impact on the trajectory of our planet because of their ability to dream for a better future. Those dreams inspired action. Those actions prompted change. Those changes resulted in improvements. Could your current financial position use a little dream power right now?

By now you may be checking the cover of the book to ensure you've purchased the right one. You bought a book about controlling your finances, but you're getting a history lesson about dreamers. That sounds about right, doesn't it? In order to become more successful in the future, we need to examine the past.

But what do the two gentlemen mentioned so far in this chapter teach us about finances? The important thing to realize is that first you have to have a dream big enough to change your life. Next, you have to be realistic and recognize that it will take good financial control to make these things happen.

Mother Teresa may be remembered as one of the simplest and most loving people to ever walk the earth, perhaps second only to Jesus. Her uniquely kind heart served the poorest of nations, but she couldn't have done it without the financial assistance of others. In a land of so little, it was crucial for her to use the resources available to her optimally.

You aren't likely to be as poor as Mother Teresa or the people around her in Calcutta, India. You also aren't likely to earn billions of dollars, like Elon Musk. But you're perfectly able to do something equal to both of these giants. You can dream, then plan and execute your dreams, regardless of where your financial scorecard ranks you right at this moment.

> If you didn't have to think about the cost, what is something you've always wanted to do?

Now that the excuses are off the table, let's take a moment to imagine that money was no object. If you didn't have to think about the cost, what is something you've always wanted to do? Go ahead, write it down. How does this assignment make you feel? If it brings up anger, disappointment, or fear, don't worry. You're not alone. Through conversations with many, I've found that most people allow money to control them, rather than the other way around.

During my thirty-plus years of personal business ownership, I can remember seasons during which money had total control of me. Those were dark days, fearful days, and certainly not the days when I loved being a business owner. If you feel that way right now, don't let it hold you a minute longer. Keep reading, expand your mind, and by the end of this book I hope you'll be able to exercise a joyful control over your finances that fills you with excitement for the future.

To complete this chapter, let's try an exercise to get your mind thinking about some possibilities for your future. If you've already read *Joyful Wealth*, this may seem familiar. I'm going to present a few sentences, and you'll need to fill in the blanks.

If it's challenging to complete these sentences, understand that it's all right to feel that way. Most do have trouble the first time they see sentences like these. This exercise is meant to begin in you the mental transformation that's necessary to take you from where you are today to where you want to be in the future. May these simple sentences transform your state of mind so that the problems you feel are significant today will vanish as you read through the remaining pages of this book.

Now grab your pen and write down your answers for future reference. Ideally, you'll want to check back on these responses from time to time, perhaps every six to twelve months, to see if you would answer any differently as time goes on.

Answer with as much detail as you can. If you get stumped, that's okay. You can skip one and come back to it later, once your creative juices start flowing.

1. If money wasn't an issue, the first thing I would do is _____.

2. If I could pick any job, it would be _____.

3. If I could donate my time to my favourite charitable cause, it would be _____.

4. If I could live anywhere in the world, it would be _____.

5. If I could drive any car I like, it would be a _____.

6. If I could vacation anywhere in the world, I would go to _____.

7. The perfect restaurant experience for me would be _____.

8. If I could take my closest friends and family on vacation with me, I would _____.

9. If time played no factor, I would _____.

Wherever possible, develop these statements with brilliant detail. Take the time to expand your responses into entire paragraphs. Include as much detail as possible until you can see, taste, or feel the statement coming to life. As you do this, your mind will begin the task of making these statements your reality.

With a vision for your new future in front of you now, we're going to lay the foundation for that vision in Chapter Two. Don't put your pencil away. Get ready to begin setting yourself up for a lifelong journey of joyful finances—starting today!

2

Building Your Base on a Strong Foundation

He is like a man which built an house, and digged deep, and laid
the foundation on a rock: and when the flood arose, the stream
beat vehemently upon that house, and could not shake it:
for it was founded upon a rock.
(Luke 6:48, KJV)

Regardless of where you wake up in the morning, or which foot you step out of bed with, there's a certain confidence that comes with knowing you have a solid floor beneath your bed. Something my wife and I enjoy doing is visiting real estate properties that are for sale. We love to dream about living in big, beautiful homes or even little fixer upper homes.

In nearly every community or neighbourhood we visit, we find a little time to stop in at an open house or just browse through the local real estate listings to see what might be available to look at. When we walk through a home, we can often tell straight away how much it's likely to be listed for, how desirable it is, and how quickly it will sell, just by walking across the floors. By doing so, we're basically doing a quick evaluation of the foundation, to see if it's solid, if it has stood the test of time.

Here's what we've learned: the more solid the foundation, the more desirable the home, the more interest is generated, the quicker the sale. By direct contrast, if the floor creaks, the corners aren't square, or there's an apparent angle as you walk from one room to the next, it becomes evident that someone didn't lay the foundation solidly. These homes are immediately less desirable, because every prospective buyer knows that an uncertain amount of work will be needed in order to straighten everything up.

When it comes to your finances, just like building a home, the most important thing is to build upon a solid foundation. We have to begin at the bottom, creating something solid to set our feet on, and then work our way up.

Many of the fundamentals were covered previously in *Joyful Wealth*, but I'll iterate the basic building blocks that are sure to get you started on the right track. If any of these ideas seem to stir your emotions, that's great!

Many of these concepts may also seem foreign to you at first, or maybe even contradictory to the things you learned in childhood. To that, I can only offer this: if you aren't entirely satisfied with your finances right now, you need to do something different in order to get to a new place. If you find yourself thinking, *But my dad always told me this* or *My mother taught me that*, then I can relate. Most of what we learn in life does come from what we witness in our parents.

> ...if you aren't entirely satisfied with your finances right now, you need to do something different in order to get to a new place.

Sadly, however, when it comes to finances, the vast majority of people in North America today get their education from credit card companies or multinational corporations that can afford thirty-second ads on TV. We need better sources of financial information than that! And since the school boards generally let us down on this subject, resources such as this book become critically important in changing the way people think about their financial future.

Throughout this book, I'll refer to money as "soldiers," and soldiers need a base to call home. In my opinion, your financial foundation is the base that your soldiers will call home.

Now, let's get started with the basic principles involved in building a solid financial base.

How You Think Affects How You Act

A lot of studies would support the idea that what you think about, you bring about. It's a phrase I first heard nearly twenty-five years ago, and to this day it rings in my head continuously. In a nutshell, it implies that if you think money is hard to come by, you will always struggle to find it. If you think good jobs are hard to find, you will be correct.

On the other hand, if you believe that money comes to you abundantly, that you have everything you need, you will also be correct.

This explains why two people can experience the exact same circumstance and yet their perspectives can be so different. Each processes the experience uniquely, filtering it through their own way of thinking. People's perceptions may be directly contrary to one another. Have you ever seen that happen where money is concerned? I see it all the time.

Born and raised in Ontario, Canada, I was blessed with an opportunity at the age of twenty-five to join a group of missionaries from our church who travelled to an impoverished region of Mexico. Our mission was to construct a school and perform some much-needed maintenance on a couple of the surrounding churches.

I returned home from that journey with a different conception of what poor looks like. I was truly a changed person. Although I've heard many people since then claim that they're broke, that they have no money, that they can't afford the flatscreen TV they want, none of them come close to the level of poorness I encountered on that trip to Mexico.

The next time you find yourself thinking "I hate my job; I work hard and am still broke" or "Why do bad things always happen to me?" be aware that these thoughts make themselves come true. Changing your thoughts, and choosing your words carefully, will have a major impact on your reality today.

Emotion Words

The first exercise I'd like to introduce you to is designed to arouse your attention to the emotional attachment you have with some common words that form the foundation of your financial base. Imagine a brick with each of the following words on them, stacked up to form a wall. Think about how you feel when you see each word.

We can start with the word "money." Did you feel something when you read it? Fear perhaps? Anger? Does it conjure up positive or negative feelings for you?

Remember that we bring about that which we think about. If you can acknowledge the feelings that are currently attached to these words, you can consciously change the way you think about them. In doing so, you'll develop the ability to change your future—just like that.

Allow me to introduce a thought about money that I, too, have carried with me for many years. It's been said that money ranks right up there with oxygen in terms of importance in life; it's not the most important thing, but it does seem that the more you have, the easier it is to breathe.

But no, it's not the most important thing. There are a lot of things in life that are more important than money—health, love, and family, just to name a few.

However, money does make life easier. Now, bear in mind that it doesn't make life *easy*. Just easier.

From my perspective, this is a wonderfully accurate summation of money. Since adopting this point of view and allowing it to park in my mind, I've come to recognize that relationships and health aren't worth jeopardizing in exchange for money.

More importantly, I refuse to believe that life isn't any good if I don't have enough money. Money doesn't make life good or bad; it only makes it a little bit better. The responsibility to build a good life is on me alone, not on how much money I have.

I hope these ideas begin to resonate with you, because it really will form a solid foundation for your financial base.

Let me take you back one more time to my trip to Mexico, where children play, smiling ear to ear, with absolutely no concept of what a bank account is. They know life is good, even without money.

Now, what about the word "budget"? How does that word make you feel? If you're anything like my wife, the word budget brings to mind a spreadsheet. Being a trained accountant, one thing that can get my wife excited is a good spreadsheet.[2] It's likely no surprise then that when someone mentions the word budget, she starts to feel a little smile building up inside her as she daydreams about the forthcoming spreadsheet, tabs, hyperlinks, and other nerdy stuff she loves to do to organize her data.

Well, we're not all accountants, right? So that word may have a totally different effect on you. When you hear it, do you think of handcuffs, someone trying to restrict your spending habits? Do you think of skyscrapers, business plans, and other big dream ideas?

For the sake of this book, the purpose of a budget is to create a heightened sense of awareness regarding where your money comes from and where it goes. By increasing your awareness of the flow of your finances, you'll gain the ability to make changes you may never have thought possible and redirect more of that money into your own pocket rather than someone else's.

---

[2] Yeah, I know, lucky me. That's all it takes to excite my wife.

The word budget is a great one for us to learn and get familiar with. If you think about it as nothing more than a way to increase your awareness, you too will soon see it as a very positive word.

How about "bank balance"? Now there's an exciting term. Imagine how much more exciting it would be if you actually had one! One that wasn't red, anyway.

If you think the balance on your loan is the kind of balance I'm referring to here, we really have a lot of work to do. Your bank balance is the amount of money you have resting in a particular account at a given point in time.

It's easy to sometimes get too caught up in the importance of a bank balance. Does it really matter if you have $100 in the bank or $100,000? Perhaps it makes a little difference, but I'll let you in on a little secret: the vast majority of wealthy people don't have big bank balances. Sure, they may have a lot of money, but it doesn't just sit in a bank account.

The next word is one I used to only associate with children, at least until I got serious about changing my financial direction. Here it is: "allowance." Some might associate the word with permission.

When was the last time you heard that word? Did your parents offer you an allowance for completing all your chores each weekend, or perhaps you offer one to your children now? Whether it brings back memories of childhood duties, most people I speak to say this word represents a variety of ideas—but none of them relate to financial freedom.

For instance, when someone is granted an allowance, they're being granted an opportunity to remove a certain barrier that's been placed on them. They're given some money they didn't have otherwise.

But there are other types of allowance. A prisoner in jail, for example, is given a freedom allowance to venture outside his or her cell for a period of time each day. Therefore, a freedom allowance offers someone an opportunity to use their time in a way they wouldn't otherwise be permitted to use it.

It would be fair to say that the word allowance can be associated with the word "privilege." If you're operating under a mindset based on lack, you may interpret this word to refer to limits or restrictions. However, to another person the same word could imply freedom and release from some form of restriction. Isn't it amazing how one word can carry such opposite interpretations?

Allowance. How does it make you feel? Do you need to change the way you interpret this word so that it can increase the joy in your life?

What about the word "donation"? This word has a large variety of different impacts on people. There are people I know who get excited by the mere thought of where they can donate next, while many others squirm at the idea of having to give away a single penny of their hard-earned money.

What feelings arise in you when you read, hear, or say the word "donate"? Do you place your hands in your pocket to protect your wallet and loose change? Do you consider the impact your money or time could have on the lives of others, perhaps people you've never met before?

Donations can come in many forms. They are often financial, because currency is so liquid and useful in so many ways, but donations can also be made in the form of time, or furniture, food, or any other type of object that can fill a person's need.

For the sake of your joyful financial future, I would like to introduce the idea that donating is possibly the greatest financial gift you will ever be invited to engage in, not just for the receiver but for you as well. We will cover this concept further later on in the book, but for now it's important to see that donations aren't reserved only for the ultra-rich. Those who have little have much to give.

Perhaps not all of these words resonate with you right now, but some are likely to produce strong emotional triggers. These emotions have a lot to do with how we act and react to our various circumstances.

For the sake of this book, we want to examine your actions as they relate to your finances. So becoming aware of what drives your decisions, or makes you act in particular ways, is a great place to start.

Additional words you may wish to say out loud so you can monitor your emotional reaction include "income," "expense," "financial statement," and "credit score." We're going to look at each of these words much more closely as we move forward, but for now just take a moment and see if they spark a feeling. Perhaps you're unsure of what they mean. That's okay.

Visual Exercise: Listing Your Emotions

If you have negative emotions attached to any of the words listed so far, or if they make you a little angry or scared, I would encourage you to make a list. Perhaps there are other words that trigger you that haven't been mentioned yet. If so, write them down, just like you do when you need to pick up a few items from the grocery store.

- •Money
- •Budget
- •Bank balance
- •Allowance
- •Donation

If you're able to recognize the emotion conjured up by the word, then write it down. For instance:

- •Money—ignorance, fear
- •Budget—control, restriction
- •Bank balance
- •Allowance
- •Donation

This exercise is for you only. No one else is going to see it, so be honest.

If you feel ignorant when it comes to money, you're certainly not alone. Very few people in the world receive a solid education when it comes to money. Through this book, I do hope that your name will be added to the list of people who understand it.

Together, we will tear down the negative emotions attached to your list of words. Our goal is to create a future for you that includes joyful finances. There's no room for negative emotions in our joyful space, so first we need to acknowledge the barriers that exist in us—if there are any—and begin to conquer them by way of learning new information, gaining an alternative perspective, and applying these lessons in a practical way.

Although it's a daunting subject, the world of finances doesn't have to be limited to trained accountants and successful businesspeople. Every single person on this planet has a financial need in order to optimize the joy they experience during their time here. With a greater awareness of how finances work, you can join the many who experience joyful finances.

Lost in Technology

With so many wonderful forms of technology available to us today, I'm reminded of my early visits to the bank. Some of you may be thinking, *You actually had to visit a bank?* That's correct. The online banking services we enjoy today are a relatively new business model. When I was a child learning how to manage my own money, visits to the bank were as common as going to the grocery store to get fresh fruit.

One of my first revenue sources began when I was just ten years old. I stumbled across an opportunity that became very lucrative, and it certainly gave me a jumpstart to my financial education. My mom or dad used to bring me to our town's bank so I could make deposits, and once I turned the money over to the teller I also had to give them my bankbook—a small book about the size of a calculator, consisting of about a dozen pages and stored in a protective plastic sleeve when not in use. The teller would open the bankbook and slide it under a printer to update my account information and bank balance.

Oh how fondly I recall those early trips to the bank. I loved to retrieve my bankbook and marvel at the $62.14 balance after making a $4.25 deposit. Those were huge numbers for me then. In my ten-year-old mind, I was the next Bill Gates.

Without even realizing it, I was learning one of the fundamentals of household banking: how to balance my bank account. Given that technology has developed so much, I don't remember how long it's been since one of those little bankbooks followed me home from the bank, so this simple practice is no longer common.

While no longer common, though, I still believe that balancing your bank-book is every bit as important as it was back then. Sadly, however, for the sake of convenience, this practice has been diluted in importance. Why take the time to balance your account when the online banking platform does it for you automatically?

To me, the answer is as obvious as asking why we bother to learn how to count now that we have calculators everywhere we go. Of course you need to learn how to count. It's a basic skill; the calculator simply allows you to manage numbers more quickly.

Balancing a bankbook is equally as fundamental as counting, and all our digital advancements should merely make it quicker for us to do it, not eliminate the need entirely.

To that point, however, I've met countless teenagers, young adults, and even men and women who try to manage their household finances while struggling to understand where all their hard-earned money has gone at the end of the week. The reason is that they have no idea how to manage their bank account.

What's the Big Idea?

In *Joyful Wealth*[3], I wrote that money is nothing but an idea. This concept was introduced to me many years ago, and it got my mind turning like never before.

To illustrate this point, I shared a story about two vacationers from different countries who tried to complete a currency exchange. Because neither one had any idea what the value of the other currency was, a deal could not be made. This is why it's so important for us to establish our thoughts about money and recognize how it affects us emotionally.

Ask yourself, what do you think money really is? To me, money is just a tool. A dollar bill is simply an "I owe you" from someone. When you hold a $10 bill in your hand, you're holding a note that says someone owes you ten dollars' worth of something.

By the conclusion of this book, I hope your concept of money will shift in a positive way, to realize that money is nothing more than a tool. Use this tool properly, and you'll be able to realize all your dreams and goals. With the proper ideas in place, you can enjoy a more joyful financial future than you've ever imagined.

The best place to start when managing your household finances is to ensure you understand where your money comes from and where it goes. Countless times I've spoken to friends about their personal circumstances only to find out that they really don't know how much money they make or what their expenses truly are. Sure, they know they make $20 per hour, or $40,000 per year, and have a mortgage obligation of $1,000 per month, but these figures paint such a broad picture of their financial position that it's not enough in order to accurately plan a joyful financial future.

The following spreadsheet has been developed as a simple to use, easy to follow tracking device for your household income and expenses throughout the year, broken down into weekly segments.[4] Every household will have a slightly different list of incomes and expenses, so I encourage you to take a few minutes to customize it to look the way it needs to in order to serve your household.

As we go through each section of the weekly entry page, make the necessary changes so that when you read the document you can get a clear picture of exactly how money flows through your home. As an example, change the heading "Income #1" to the name of the company you work for. Going forward, you can look at this line item and know exactly what the figure beside it represents.

---

[3] Connect with Ryan and learn more about his books by finding The Joyful Series on Facebook.
[4] For a downloadable version of the entire annual workbook, visit us on Facebook at The Joyful Series and start using your very own tool today, for free.

As we look at each line, mark it with the appropriate heading for your household. If your situation changes, such as if you change your job to work for another company, you can update the spreadsheet accordingly.

Keeping accurate records is a key skill in the development of a strong financial position. Those who put their heads in the sand in the hopes that everything will turn out great when they hit retirement age all too often discover that joyful finances have eluded them their whole lives. Take control. You have the tools. You just have to use them.

This is a typical weekly entry page.

Week Ending 5-Jan		EXPENSES	$$	RUNNING TOTALS
		Mortgage / Rent		
Starting Bank Balance		Loan Pymt #1	_____	New Bank Balance
		Loan Pymt #2	_____	
		Car Pymt	_____	
INCOME SOURCES	$$	Credit Line	_____	Loan #1
		Credit Card	_____	
Income #1		H&V Insurance	_____	
Income #2	_____	Vehicle Maintenance	_____	Loan #2
Extra Income #1	_____	Fuel	_____	
Extra Income #2	_____	Internet / Cable	_____	
		Phone Bills	_____	Car Loan
TOTAL INCOME	_____	Dining Out	_____	
		Groceries	_____	
Additional credit facility use	_____	Utilities	_____	Credit Card
		Charitable Donations	_____	
		Personal Withdraw #1	_____	
		Personal Withdraw #2	_____	Credit Line
		Special Occasions	_____	
		House Expenses	_____	
		Bank Chrgs & Int.	_____	Family Vacation Fund
		Family Vacation Fund	_____	
		Investment Contribution	_____	
		Miscellaneous	_____	
			_____	
			_____	
			_____	
		TOTAL EXPENSES	_____	

Note first that this page is used to track the balance of your primary household account. In the event that you have multiple bank accounts, you may choose to balance each one using this tool, but you may need a separate copy for each account, or modify this sheet to reflect the additional accounts you carry.

For the sake of simplicity, in *Joyful Wealth* we looked at opening a household account that you could use as a funnel for all the money that comes in and out of the household. We called it the Bill Payer Account, and every penny that came into the household was deposited into it. Once the income was accounted for, each expense was also accounted for, including a couple of additional items such as allowances, savings, etc.

You may wish to do the same as you get started here.

For the more advanced user, having separate entry pages for each account may work best. Perhaps a little creative customization will offer you the ability to track all your accounts on one page. This workbook is a tool, so use it in whatever way you feel most comfortable with, and in whichever way makes the information easiest for you to process. Everyone is different, and so your personal tracking sheets will be different, too.

Now, note that directly below the Week Ending line is one that says "Starting Bank Balance." If your week ending date was Saturday, January 5, for instance, the starting balance you would write down here would be the same as the closing balance from the Saturday before that, which in this case would have been Saturday, December 29.

Perhaps the balance on that afternoon was $1,010.50. If so, that's the figure you would insert on the starting balance line. It's the amount of money you have at the beginning of the week, the starting figure from which all the income and expenses will be added or subtracted in order to arrive at the new bank balance at the end of the current week.

The second step to filling out the weekly entry page is to record the income you have generated that week. For most, this is an enjoyable step. You get to insert any money you have received. The list can include items such as employment income, business income, side job income, interest/dividend/royalty income, government-provided income, etc.

Again, I encourage you to edit the headings to accurately reflect your sources so that when you review this document it's clear where the monies came from.

Beneath your list of income sources, there is a space where you can write down your total combined income. The figures we're using in this exercise are after taxes, so for the purposes of filing your income tax at the end of the year, you will simply need to produce these weekly entry pages and your respective income forms to the person who files your taxes for you. This will make the process much easier and more accurate.

Do you have other sources of income that aren't listed? No problem, add them in. We want to ensure that we capture all the money coming into the house so we can manage those funds most effectively.

One concern that has arisen for many households in recent years has been access to credit. Have you ever thought to yourself, *Shoot, I don't have enough money right now so I'll just put it on the card and pay it off next time I get paid?* We'll discuss the power of credit as a tool later in this book.

To ensure that you're aware of how much you're using your credit card, there is a line item to account for credit card purchases.

Collectively, the money you receive from your job, business, and investments represents your total household income. This is the amount of money you should strive to operate within. If you're trying to improve your lifestyle and build a strong financial foundation for the future, one initial goal should be to avoid the temptation to enlist credit when you lack funds. This includes credit cards, of course, but also lines of credit.

There is a time and place for such resources, but they shouldn't be used habitually to supplement a shortfall in your cashflow.

Where Does the Money Go?

In the centre of this spreadsheet is a column cataloguing your expenses. This column has been placed in the middle by design, because for most people this is the column that's going to require the most attention. Its real purpose is to heighten your awareness of where all of your money goes each week.

I have a friend who makes $20 per hour at her job, and she works forty hours per week. During a discussion one evening, she said to me, "I know I make $800 every week, but other than my rent and car payment, I only buy my groceries and bare necessities and then I have no idea where the rest of my money goes."

Ever been there? I know I have.

Would you like to know a little secret which took me a really long time to believe? It doesn't matter how much money you make. In fact, the more money you make, the less aware most people become regarding where it goes.

Another friend once said to me, "If you have $5,000 in cash sitting in your pocket one day, and you stop to buy a $5 burger somewhere, you really wouldn't even notice, would you?"

Of course not. That big wad would still be a big wad.

But the reality is that when you drop $5 here and another $5 there, before you know it, a big bite is taken from your initial stack. I've often heard this called being "nickelled and dimed to death."

Perhaps you've noticed how big businesses have used this tactic so brilliantly? If you have a bank account, undoubtedly you've had this happen to you. You open your bank statement and find that they charged you seventy-five cents because you sneezed while opening the statement, and $1.50 because you sent an email transfer, and another $1.50 because you have too many bills to pay but rather than going to the teller and using up their time, in a building that requires electricity and maintenance, you decided to do it from home, by yourself. Voila, there it is, another petty little charge.

Do you bother to fight all these little charges? If you have $50,000 in the bank, you might think to yourself, *Well, it's no big deal. It's not worth the time.* On the other hand, if you live paycheque to paycheque, you need those $3 to ensure that your next car payment clears. If so, then you make a call and get those fees reduced, if not entirely eliminated.

So what's the point here? Should we challenge all the little parasites attacking our finances every day, week, or month? Absolutely we should, if for no reason other than principle. But to most who don't use a tracking system for their finances, these costs eat away at their financial joy—and they aren't even aware of it. This leaves the hard-working, income-earning labourer frustrated, and even desperate at times, wandering aimlessly toward a retirement that may never arrive because there are too many unnoticed bloodsuckers.

Please take the necessary time to itemize your weekly expenses in as much detail as possible. Start with the examples we've provided, customizing them to fit your own situation.

Among the expenses listed on our page are some you may not have thought about before, such as personal withdrawals, a family vacation fund, and investment contributions.

Earlier in this chapter, we discussed words that trigger our emotions. The term "personal withdrawal" is my effort to remove the emotion that might otherwise be accompanied by the word "allowance." Essentially, a personal withdrawal is the amount of money you permit yourself to withdraw from your household income each week, for the purposes of guilt-free spending.

I strongly encourage that you keep this number very low at the beginning of your budgeting process. A great place to start would be $50 to $100 per week. The reason for this recommendation is that as you begin to get your financial situation under control, you learn to be accountable for your spending habits—and personal withdrawals are essentially opportunities to spend without any accountability. Do you want to take a friend out for lunch, get your hair coloured, or buy a motorcycle? The specific reason for the expense doesn't matter, nor does it have to be justified. If you've saved up the necessary funds, you can decide to spend it. You have no one to answer to. For that reason, this is a luxury expense, albeit one that's critical to include. Nonetheless, it should be very tightly administered in the beginning, so as not to impede your overall goals.

Saving money for your family vacations and tracking your investment contributions may be new to your budget, but they're incredibly important if you want to have a joyful future. Without taking these into consideration, you may fail to take vacations or only begin saving for retirement late in life.

If you don't save for vacations, you may end up going on a trip and paying for it with credit. And you may justify this by saying to yourself, "I work hard all year. I deserve it!" Do you, though? Do you really deserve to have to deal with an expensive credit card balance the month after you get back? Of course not.

Starting now, we can be sure to avoid that sort of scenario. Wouldn't that trip to the amusement park be a whole lot more enjoyable if you didn't have to keep paying for it the following Christmas?

So fill in all your expense figures so that you can form a clearer picture of where all your money has been going. At the bottom of the expenses column, you'll see a line where you can enter your total. If your expenses are lower than your income, you're fortunate. All too often, that's not the case. Many people discover through this process that although they work tirelessly, they're actually getting further and further into debt with each passing week. That can all stop now if you take the time to work with this tool and learn to incorporate it into your day-to-day life.

Now let's move on to the column on the right side of the page. I personally find this column to be the most enjoyable one to track week in and week out. This column consists of balances for various accounts you already have.

The first line is reserved for your new bank balance. We sure would love to see that number get bigger and bigger each week, but that isn't always the case.

Several of the lines directly below the new bank balance are related to various creditors you may have. This would include items such as loan balances, lines of credit, or mortgages. If you have a mortgage, you'll need the assistance of an amortization chart in order to track the principal remaining on the loan; this will show you how much of your weekly payment has gone towards the principal and how much has gone towards interest.

We'll certainly go into much greater detail about mortgage management later in the book.

The final two lines in the right-hand column allow you to track how much money you've accumulated in your vacation and investment funds. Obviously there's joy in seeing a vacation fund creep closer to its destination. Every week, those are the first totals you'll likely look at.

Whether you're putting aside $25 or $250 per week, there is joy in saving for a vacation. The important thing is that you'll come to look forward to completing and reviewing this tracking sheet. What if you were able to look at the bottom right of the sheet and see that you had accumulated $5,000 in investment savings this year? Do you think that would inspire you to stay on track?

Anyone who takes their financial situation into their own hands has hope for the future. Stop trying to guess where you may end up one day, afraid that you may have to work until you're in your eighties. Manage the details now, set some clear goals, track your progress every single week, and joyful finances will take shape right before your eyes—and in a much shorter timeframe than you may think.

It's hard to measure the power of seeing your progress on paper, because it has such a tremendous impact on the mind. Convince your mind that you're no longer a slave to the almighty dollar, that you're achieving a great financial destiny and your goals are coming true. When you've done that, you'll wake up with new excitement each day, revitalized by your new hope. That's what I call joyful finances.

Filling in the Figures

Now that you have an understanding of what the entire spreadsheet consists of, the part that's missing is your personal figures. Take your time with this step because it may be one of the most revealing exercises in your life. As you begin to fill in the blanks, not only will you be giving yourself an accurate account of your household finances, you'll be setting the foundation for your weekly, monthly, and annual budget.

You may be surprised when you begin to think of having an annual budget, because let's face it, haven't budgets always been reserved for large corporations with lots of money? Perhaps people associate budgeting with large companies in direct relation to their personal ability to track their budgets. If it can work for major companies such as Ford or Amazon, why wouldn't it work for someone like you? Of course it will. You simply need to implement it in a simple, easy to follow manner.

Start today, take your time, and be honest about your situation. You, too, will soon see great things begin to happen with your finances.

3

*Don't love money; be satisfied with what you have. For God has
said, "I will never fail you. I will never abandon you."*
(Hebrews 13:5, NLT)

In the previous chapter, we discussed credit cards and tracked them in the same column as one's income. But make no mistake about it: credit cards are most certainly not a source of income. Credit is more like a saw hanging on the wall of a carpenter's workshop. To the trained user, many beautiful and desirable creations may be made by this tool, but to the inexperienced, unknowledgeable, uninformed tool handler, danger lurks with every touch. To that person, it's not a matter of whether they'll get hurt, it's a matter of when—and how much pain it will cause. Credit card companies know this. In fact, they count on it.

What if you knew with absolute certainty that all you had to do is give away fifty $1 coins and in return you would be given $400? How far would you go to get rid of those coins, and how quickly would you get it done? That's essentially the golden formula for credit companies. You see, their money is powerless unless they lend it to someone. Statistics have proven that the majority of credit card holders have no idea of the dangers. All the credit company needs to do is get one of their cards into a person's hands, and then wait for history to repeat itself, again and again.

Imagine a room with one hundred people in it. They're average folks, meaning that approximately ninety-five percent of them are living paycheque to paycheque, four are financially independent, and just one person in the room is wealthy.

Based on those averages, you can imagine the room wouldn't contain an overwhelming amount of joy. The vast majority of the people are either scared or unsure of what their financial future will look like. Each guest has what they need to enjoy life, but failing to acknowledge it, they desire for more than they have and can't figure out how to obtain it.

Along comes a company… we'll call them Credit4U. This company enters the room with enthusiasm and encouragement, claiming to have the solution that will bring every single person present increased joy and happiness instantly, regardless of where they are financially today. Credit4U says they will begin by handing out these little plastic cards, all the while chanting with excitement, "No more waiting! Have the life you want today!"

The atmosphere in the room shifts entirely! Hope returns to people's eyes for the first time in years. The dreams they've kept shelved for decades suddenly return with a new sense of expectation and anticipation—dreams of new homes, big trucks, fast boats, flatscreen televisions, and trips to foreign corners of the world.

The doors of this room fly open as the guests move swiftly to their vehicles and head out in every direction possible, all armed with their new plastic dreammakers.

What's going on here? How do you think Credit4U feels the moment the gathering concludes? How should they feel? Did they not just restore lost excitement to a room full of hardworking, financially struggling, hopeless people? Sure they did, and you can bet that the representatives of this company have big ole smiles on their faces as the crowd flees and they forecast the profit soon to follow.

Is that wrong? Has Credit4U done anything dishonest, immoral, or illegal? Not really. What they've done here is take advantage of the statistics that support their business model. They know that nearly no one in that room had been educated in the proper and safe use of credit, the tool they just handed out. They know most people will misuse it and become dependent on it, much like an addict.

During the company's presentation of these magical plastic keys with the power to unlock people's deeply repressed dreams, they may have failed to mention one small disclaimer: misuse of this tool could lead to a lifelong battle with your future credit and credit score, and be accompanied by burdensome payments that will outlive the joy of the purchase you've made.

Our helpful friends at Credit4U understand the power their tools truly have. When they were handing them out—and they continue to hand them out everywhere they can, to almost anyone who will take one—they knew that the trends were strongly in their favour.

Seventy-eight percent of these shoppers will overextend themselves and not be able to make the full balance payment at the end of the month, thus exposing themselves to high interest rates. Their formula is simple: give a dollar, and expect three or four in return. So they look for creative ways to entice buyers to take their dollar as fast and as often as they can. The more dollars Credit4U hands out, the more they can rake in.

It almost sounds cruel, doesn't it?

How to Use Credit to Your Advantage

Enough about the doom and gloom of credit cards. This book is about joyful finances and the last few paragraphs have been anything but joyful.

Credit can, however, have a positive impact on the joy in our lives, as it can help create a better financial position for people who are educated in how it works. When applied properly, credit can drastically enhance one's joyful financial future.

Let's take an opportunity to examine the other side of the coin, to see what the rich and financially educated part of society understands about credit. These are the things credit card companies are perhaps a little more reluctant to share because it may affect their profit.

The word credit really means to advance something to someone. For the sake of this discussion, we're most typically referring to cash, meaning that a person is being advanced cash to purchase something.

Until the mid 1990s, obtaining credit required a visit to the bank and generally involved some begging and grovelling in order to convince the banker to approve your loan request. Due to the effort involved, most credit requests were reserved for purchases of great expense—people seeking to acquire homes or cars.

Today, as part of the evolution of North American consumerism, retailers have recognized the advantage of advancing smaller amounts of money to people. Suddenly, people who dream of a bigger television or new sofa no longer need to wait. Even retailers began issuing credit. Before long, consumers were able to use credit to purchase everything from clothing to televisions. Even groceries could be purchased on credit. You no longer have to save up for your next great purchase; you can have it now.

What other benefits could people realize under this new business model? Convenience. Aren't we all in search of a more convenient lifestyle to bring us more joy? Sure we are. Fast food drive thru lanes are clear indicators of this.

So it should be no surprise that when retailers started advancing credit, allowing consumers to bypass the bank, an entirely new level of convenience arrived. People everywhere embraced this new time-saving purchasing power, unaware of its pitfalls.

Instant gratification and a more convenient lifestyle. Boy, if credit did nothing more for a consumer, one would have to argue that these two benefits alone would tip the scales, encouraging everyone to go out and get as much credit as they can.

Well, crazy as it may sound, the more you understand the benefits of credit, the more you begin to understand how close to the truth this actually is. But there needs to be a big disclaimer here: every consumer needs to be educated about the benefits and pitfalls of credit. Becoming aware of how credit works increases one's ability to capitalize on its perks and decreases the seduction that can lead to long-term financial burdens.

> ...every consumer needs to be educated about the benefits and pitfalls of credit.

The Benefits of Credit

Loyalty points. The easiest perk to understand comes in the form of customer loyalty points, so we'll start there. Walk into nearly any big box store and someone with a clipboard and lanyard around their neck will be sure to be trolling the aisles.

"Do you have the store-sponsored credit card that instantly gets you twenty thousand points just for signing up and an additional three points for every dollar you spend today?"

The college-bound salesperson approaches customer after customer, trying to hook them by giving away tens of thousands of points right out of the gate. These points accumulate with your spending and hopefully, one day, they can amount to something valuable.

And they can. In 2011, these points accumulated so nicely that my wife and I enjoyed our first trip as newlyweds on the credit card company's dime. This wasn't just one of those three-day getaways either. We spent eight days at the famous Turtle Bay Resort in Hawaii, golfed some amazing oceanside courses, and even took a helicopter tour around the island of Oahu. How's that for a credit card perk? It was the trip of a lifetime really, courtesy of Visa.

Whether you use your credit card points to take a trip somewhere tropical or purchase groceries, it's an obvious benefit that's easy to understand and take advantage of. The benefit is available to all credit card users without additional qualifications or skills; you simply have to ensure that the card you choose offers some form of points.

Membership discounts. Some retailers are even more committed to their plastic money. Rather than simply offering every user the same number of points based solely on purchase volume or frequency, they also offer exclusive discounts. Costco, Kohl's, and Meijer come to mind as retailers that are willing to reduce the price at which they sell you their products, provided you charge the purchase to one of their convenient credit cards.

Have you ever wondered how they can do that? It's rather simple math.

These big stores have done enough research that they know the chances of someone not paying their balance in full is pretty high. Really high, in fact. So they offer a two, three, or maybe even five percent discount on purchases made using their card, encouraging the buyer to charge it. This causes people to justify making larger purchases as they consider not only the points they will earn but also the savings from the discounts offered. It's savings on top of savings, right? Who could pass that up?

The retailer appears to be giving their merchandise away, but they're actually trying to hook you. Around the fifteenth of the next month, you open your credit card statement and find that you have a brand-new balance of $1,200, due in a week.

Yikes! What did we buy that cost that much? Your thoughts begin to race. *Okay, I've got this. We can pay $600 this month and $600 next month, and it will be gone. We can do that.*

And just like that, the benefit of the savings and points has escaped you by way of unplanned interest charges. With the average interest rate on a credit card being 15.99 percent, compounding monthly, you could be facing hundreds of dollars in interest the moment you miss that first payment in full. To capitalize on the true benefits of credit card purchasing, as it relates to points or membership discounts, it's crucial that you monitor and control your spending so that you can make the payment in full at the end of each billing cycle. Anything less, and you're just taking out a very expensive loan from a ruthless lender.

Leverage. Anytime there are reduced prices or added points related to your spending, the benefit is fairly easy to recognize and calculate. This is why retailers use them as bait: they're appetizing to nearly every consumer. There is, however, a benefit that's much less commonly understood or recognized—and for the sake of achieving joyful finances, it's one you need to understand. It applies to many areas of successful living, and once understood it contains the power to realize results much greater than a person can accomplish singlehandedly.

This benefit is called *leverage.* Leverage may be the oldest tool in the history of mankind. Nearly anything of significance that has ever been achieved has been done through the use of leverage.

One of the greatest examples dates back to the times of the Egyptian pyramids. Documentary after documentary has been produced on these amazing constructions. It's said that the sheer size and weight of the building blocks would pose challenges even to modern-day engineering and construction teams. Yet with the use of levering tools—mainly pulley systems—man was able to multiply the strength of a thousand people and in turn raise some of the most wondrous and mysterious buildings ever built.

All right, perhaps you'll never find a pulley to reel in the pile of money you think you need to make your life better, but the same concept can be applied to your finances. Rather than ropes, though, you can use credit.

How would that work, exactly?

To start, we have to be sure we understand what leverage really means. In its most basic form, it simply means to do more with less. That's leverage. Simple, right?

Many corporations have interpreted this to mean they can get more productivity with fewer people. Most have found that this isn't a sustainable implementation of leverage. It may work in the short-term, but it's not exactly what I have in mind.

Doing more with less means that you have to figure out ways to multiply your results without having to increase your effort. There are lots of ways this can be done. Technology has been a key for people wanting to leverage themselves, and perhaps the most common way is to simply hire people to do what you want done. More results, less effort, equals leverage.

And then there's credit.

Billy and Ted were having a conversation about credit leveraging when Billy suggested, "Just borrow some money, and you'll be rich."

The puzzled look on Ted's face left no room for misinterpretation. "So you want me to go into debt, and you think that's going to help me get rich? Have you lost your marbles? I came over to talk about how I could get myself out of debt, Billy! That's my problem. I don't make enough money each month to make the payments for all the debt I have now."

"Hear me out, Ted," Billy said to his desperate friend. "You're a hard-working guy, no question about it, but you're just one guy. You put in your hours and get a paycheque. And then what? You use your money to buy what you need to enjoy life, but there doesn't seem to be enough. Seems to me you have three choices here. First, you could obviously spend less, but I get it—you've cut back a bunch already and it simply hasn't been enough. Second, you could work more than you do, but that comes at the risk of ruining relationships in your life, and ruining your health, so that's not a great option either. Third, you could look at what credit might be available to you so you can start buying assets that put money in your pocket each month rather than taking it out. Does that make any sense?"

As their conversation continued, Billy explained to Ted that the reason he was in his current situation was that he was acting like a one-man show. He spent everything he made, and perhaps a little more at times, on liabilities. His money wasn't working for him at all. Because of all his bills, he didn't have any money left over to put to work. The only solution was to put other people's money to work.

That's what leverage is. Getting more results without additional effort—and we will certainly be looking further into assets, liabilities, and leverage as we continue throughout this book.

I once overheard a conversation at a real estate investment workshop I attended. In fact, this same conversation is heard at almost every real estate seminar I've ever attended.

The basic principle goes like this. If you have $10,000 to invest and you want to purchase stocks, almost all investors will be able to purchase $10,000 worth of stocks. But if you decide to invest your money in real estate, lenders are more likely to offer you the opportunity to purchase much more—for example, as much as $100,000 in real estate.

Again, that's leverage. In both cases, you have worked the same amount to save $10,000. Through financing, however, there's a way to increase the amount of money that goes to work for you.

The important thing, no matter what your source of credit, is that no matter how much you borrow, or how much you pay for the money you borrow, you have to understand cashflow. Ask yourself this question: is the cost of borrowing less than the return on your investment? If the answer is yes, then you're successfully leveraging your money and/or someone else's money.

Let's look at a few examples.

Imagine that you decide to purchase some RRSPs, because you're going to retire one day and your financial advisor has suggested that they're easy and affordable to purchase. He says that you can invest as little as one hundred dollars at a time, anytime you want. So throughout the year, you make modest investments as often as you can.

Then you get a call right before income tax season and your very proactive financial advisor says, "Joe, I've got some great news for you! You've been doing a terrific job putting away money this year, and because of this you're in a wonderful position to take advantage of an amazing opportunity. The government just issued a notice that if you put $5,000 into a specific fund, they'll give you a forty percent tax credit straight away. This means you essentially get $2,000 back for making a $5,000 investment. How great is that for return on investment?"

Before you can respond, he adds one thing: "You're just $1,000 short of the maximum contribution, so I wanted to call you right away and encourage you to top up the account so you can take full advantage."

Since you started this process, you've been giving him everything you could afford to give—and now he thinks you're just going to reach between the couch cushions and pull out a cool $1,000?

You want to say, *Get real, man.*

But instead you reply, "Yeah, that does sound awesome. But I just don't have that extra money right now. I'm going to have to pass."

And like more than ninety-nine percent of your fellow investors, you're ready to hang up the phone and head off to another day at the office so you can keep saving at the pace you're on, which makes a turtle's pace seem like fast-forward.

He doesn't let you hang up the phone, though.

"Hold on, Joe," your advisor says. "I know you've been good with your money, and you've been investing what you can. Let me ask you this: do you have a credit card that you could possibly take a $1,000 advance from?"

Feeling like this is becoming a pushy sales pitch, you reluctantly say, "Probably." But you want to hang up immediately.

"Joe, listen. If you take an advance for $1,000, even if the interest rate is 19.99 percent annually, you're going to get $2,000 back in about six weeks. You can use those funds to pay off the credit card in full and still have some extra money to invest further. Don't you see? You can't afford *not* to borrow the money."

Maybe you're reading this right now and thinking, *No way. That doesn't happen. That's just a story.* But I'm telling you that conversations like that happen every single day.

Because of how popular it is in our North American culture to think of credit as a means to make an immediate purchase, the vast majority of people overlook it as a leveraging tool when it comes to investments.

Credit cards are very powerful tools that offer many wonderful opportunities. Sadly, consumerism is generally much more influential than sound financial advice. Sure, you're reading this book right now and the pages are full of positive food for your financial diet, but how often do you read material such as this? Now compare that frequency with how often you see an ad that persuades you to believe a product is the only thing between you and increased happiness.

If your financial diet is filled with advertisements, you need to combat it with the financial intelligence that will take you into the future. At a minimum, your education will provide you with the basis of joyful finances. Whether that brings you to the final destination of your dreams, only time and discipline will tell.

I want to wrap up this section by encouraging you not to be afraid of credit cards and borrowing money. Rather, educate yourself about the power of credit to assist you with leveraging your efforts so you can multiply your results in life.

Most people simply hear the word credit and start to shut down. If you find out someone is willing to lend you credit, take it as a compliment that they're willing to give you their money to invest. Search for opportunities that would allow you to borrow their money for less than it costs to invest. For example, a lender may give you a mortgage at five percent and you can buy a property that earns back ten percent.

We're going to learn later why this is such a wonderful exchange. Fortunes have been made using this simple philosophy.

How Does Your Credit Score Measure Up?

Perhaps the best place to start is to simply explain what a credit score is. To begin with, if you've ever opened an account with a creditor that reports to the credit bureau, you have a score, whether you realize it or not.

Generally you need to be eighteen years of age in order to open a credit card or get a loan at the bank, so that's when your score begins. Most people under the age of eighteen are unlikely to have any credit score at all.

Common lines of credit that often initiate a credit score include credit cards, student loans, mortgages, car loans, or personal loans. If you went to college at age seventeen and applied for and were approved to receive a student loan or a college credit card, you may find out that your credit was being scored even before you knew what it was.

So what is it and how is it calculated? Several companies track your credit score. The two most popular at the time this book was written are Equifax and TransUnion. Recently, however, a website called Credit Karma has emerged as an exceptionally convenient and free way to check your score. These companies analyze your payment history, determine how much debt you have, and see how long you've been using credit. They plug all that data into a complicated matrix and spit out a score.

The scores range from 300 to 900, although many say that 850 is considered perfect credit because there are too many variables to actually achieve 900.

Why is this score so important?

Companies like Credit Karma, Equifax, and TransUnion are able to produce reports detailing your credit history. Until recently, people have had to pay a nominal fee to retrieve these reports, but now they're available almost anywhere, anytime, at no cost. The reports indicate how much credit has been extended to you, who has extended that credit, how much the payments are, and how consistent you are at making the payments on time. They also include information regarding delinquent payments, defaulted loans, bankruptcies, and even how many accounts you've closed out. If someone is considering lending you money for any reason, be it a car dealership, mortgage lender, or credit card company, they'll find one of these reports and use it to make their determination.

Today, we hear so many stories about identity theft and fraud. Let's face it—with the amount of electronic interaction that's permitted today, you can apply for a credit card online in about fifteen minutes on any number of sites. Who's to say that the information that gets posted to your credit report, which ultimately determines your credit score, is accurate? Only you can tell that.

I want to encourage you, even if you have no need for credit today, to find out what your report and score are to ensure that someone hasn't accidentally filed a $25,000 credit card account against your name. And if you happen to have an old department store credit line, with a company such as Sears, for instance, that's no longer in business and you know you'll never use that card again, find out who the issuer of that credit is and close the account. Not only is that a good practice so you can rest assured no one will steal the card and successfully charge a balance against it, it's also helpful in terms of increasing your score. And should you need credit one day, it will be more available to you.

One false belief about credit scores is that you'll improve your score by having four different credit cards that you never use. While having a credit card is a wonderful step towards improving your score, it's the disciplined use and timely payment of monthly balances that improves your score, not simply having an open account that never gets used.

On the contrary. If you have credit that you don't use, it actually reduces the amount of credit a future lender will be willing to provide. A lender will take into consideration the availability of credit on those accounts and whether you've used it or not. If you still have access to all the credit on your report, a lender will perceive that as potentially dangerous.

Let me explain. If you have five department store credit cards that you haven't used in ten years—and in fact, you may not even know where they are anymore—and each one has a $1,000 credit limit, then you appear to have access to $5,000. Despite carrying zero balances on these cards for as long as anyone can remember, when you step into the dealership to discuss financing for that beautiful new vehicle you've been dreaming about for three years, you may be disappointed to find out that the leader won't give you the amount you were expecting, because you already have access to that $5,000. Although you thought you would have no problem getting a loan for $20,000, and the dealership is in total agreement that you could support that loan, lending you that amount would require you to actually be able to support loans of $25,000. Your credit report will have suggested to them that you might be stretched too thin if that actually happened.

So cut out the fat. If you no longer use a card, or don't foresee the need to use a line of credit that was previously extended to you and which you paid off, close the account today. It will protect you from fraud and give you access to more money should you need it at a later time. Having credit sitting dormant has a negative impact on your future borrowing ability. While leaving it open and unused won't impact your credit score directly, it does limit how much you can borrow when you need to, so you have nothing to lose by closing old accounts.

Another misbelief I often hear is "I had an issue with Company XYZ and now my credit score is wrecked for life."

In the moment, doesn't it always feel like things are never going to get better? A married couple celebrates their fiftieth anniversary on a Saturday, and while having breakfast on Monday they begin to argue about which item on their menu Saturday night was the best. Suddenly he thinks to himself, *She always has to argue with me. I'm never right.* Perhaps there's some truth to his thought, but in the heat of the argument he is able to forget that she's been by his side for the best fifty years of his life.

Well, in the same way, the credit companies will eventually forgive and forget. Even if you once suffered the experience of a bankruptcy, depending on the type, your credit report will forget that information within seven to ten years.

So don't give up hope. As time goes on, you can begin to rebuild your credit by doing the small things that matter. As soon as possible, obtain a low-balance credit card and use it routinely with discipline, ensuring to pay the balance on time at the end of each month, in full. Pay your rent, utilities, or any other bills on time, every time. This will confirm your diligence in rebuilding your credit. It may not be easy, and it may not happen overnight, but I assure you that time is an amazing healer.

Protect your credit well enough and one day you might find yourself using your card to make big purchases—like buying a home in a foreign country.

Plenty of times in our lives, opportunities are missed, not because we cannot afford to take them, but because we lack access to liquid cash. Credit cards provide that resource, and in direct proportion to how well you've managed your credit card privileges, you will have the power to capitalize on investment opportunities that others may not.

Say you happen to be out for a Sunday drive. You and your spouse have been talking about some kind of real estate investment, but you've never really gotten serious about it. One thing that scares you is the idea that you have to put up $10,000 to $50,000 in order to qualify for a mortgage, and then you'll have this looming debt to pay and what if the tenants don't work out, and so on and so on.

As you're driving, you spot an elderly woman, Ms. Betty, whom you've met in town many times before. You notice she's struggling to carry a large item to the road. You're not in any particular hurry, so you decide to stop and lend a hand.

Ms. Betty is very tired and says that she'll soon be moving into a retirement home and is trying to clean out her house. Frightened by the prospect of having to find a realtor she can trust and worried about all the hassle that will come from emptying the house and selling it, she makes this casual comment: "I just wish I knew someone who wanted to take this house from me."

In the back of your mind, you replay the conversation you've been having with your spouse.

Hmmm, you think. *I wonder if this place would be a good starter?*

"Oh dear," Ms. Betty says. "There's so much stuff to get rid of here. If only someone would take the house as is for $25,000, because I'm just too tired to do all this work by myself."

If you think this scenario is too fictitious to be true, I can tell you from personal experience that opportunities like it come up from time to time. Luck, they say, is when opportunity meets preparedness.

So how can having a really good credit history help you create your own luck? Well, before this couple left Ms. Betty's house that day, they had agreed to purchase her home, complete with all the stuff she didn't want to have to haul away, for $25,000. On Monday, as soon as the banks reopened from the weekend, they planned to take out a cash advance on their credit card to provide her with the money.

Lucky for them, they had built their credit strong and always made their required payments, so they had access to cash when they needed it to capitalize on an opportunity. Had they not been prepared, how do you think this story would have been remembered years later?

"Oh man, there was a house we should have bought but just couldn't come up with the money fast enough," they might say. "The seller only wanted $25,000 and the house would be worth $100,000 today, but we screwed up on our credit a few times, didn't have access to that kind of money, and then some rich guy came and scooped up our deal."

Ever heard that story before?

Do you have to be rich to have access to large amounts of cash? Absolutely not, and $25,000 is certainly not a large amount—unless, of course, you need $25,000 and don't have access to it. Then it's a whole lot.

So building credit is a wonderful way to work towards wealth, because you really don't need to have a lot of money to build up your credit.

The second thing to see here is that the buyer didn't need to have money to make money. The buyer used someone else's money to purchase the home, taking advantage of the trustworthiness they had established over time. Trustworthiness is *free* to build, for the record.

Lastly, if you're like me, you might ask this question: what about the new credit card balance these buyers now had to pay every month?

Great question. Let's see what we might be able to do with that.

To start with, what would be the minimum monthly payment on a $25,000 credit card balance at 19.99 percent interest? The answer is around $300. To get into this deal, it would be crucial that you be able to afford to make this $300 payment on time each month, because you certainly wouldn't want to jeopardize the credibility you've established to get into this position in the first place.

Now, no one wants to pay 19.99 percent interest on anything for very long, even if it's a tax-deductible investment expense. So how do we eliminate the high-interest loan? What we've come to learn is that refinancing a home is infinitely less challenging than buying a home in the first place, especially if there's equity in the property.

For the purpose of our example, it's possible that you could approach the bank the day after holding title to the property and request a mortgage. Depending on your relationship with them, they may even offer to pay for the appraisal. Remember, credit card debt is more expensive because it's not guaranteed by any assets. This means that when you approach the bank, you're asking them to lend you money on a house that has no attached debt. In other words, they would see that the title is free and clear or there is no lien.

In one case for me and my wife, a home we purchased was believed to be worth more than four times the original purchase price. The bank agreed to lend us fifty percent of the estimated value, site unseen, without an appraisal. The whole thing was based merely on a banker's opinion.

Back to our couple with the $25,000 home purchase. When they go to the bank, it's possible the bank would offer them a $50,000 mortgage or home equity line of credit without ever visiting the property. The interest rate with the bank would likely be around three to five percent for them, based on their credit. And perhaps if the couple elected to accept the terms on a $40,000 loan at four percent, they would have enough money to pay off the credit card in full—gaining huge points with the credit card lender, because it further demonstrates their responsibility to manage credit. They would also then have some working capital (additional money) to clean the house, fix it up, and either get it ready for rent or sale. The new monthly payment on this loan would be around $125, and it would be partially tax-deductible because it's an investment expense.

Let's say the couple takes three months to clean the property and sell it. Fixed up, let's say that the property sells for $95,000. With a quick close and before the fourth payment is due on the loan, the lawyers close the sale and our young couple have just made a sale profit of nearly $50,000.

It should be noted here that the only out-of-pocket costs the couple incurred in this scenario were the three payments of $125. However, if any portion of the refinanced $40,000 loan was available to make those payments, then this $50,000 profit would be an excellent example of someone who used other people's money to make money for themselves. It squashes the old saying that you need to have money to make money.

There are a lot of things you can do to put yourself in a position to have an experience like this, and it takes time. Managing your credit is a very practical way to develop a solid financial foundation for wealth.

Summing It Up

Remember the example of the saw hanging on the wall of the carpenter's workshop? With a tool like that, you can create something beautiful—if you're educated and skilled in its use. If not, danger and harm could be the consequence.

For most consumers, their lack of understanding about the benefits of credit leads to a lifetime of financial struggle, difficult monthly payments, and countless interest charges that can maintain a relentless chokehold on them.

Credit cards can be used for a lot more than covering your purchases until payday. The proper cards can be used to get price reductions, collect points, and even employ leverage towards investing in your future.

The moment you activate your first credit card, your credit history begins to write itself on your credit report. These reports are used to calculate a credit score that reflect your personal habits regarding borrowing and paying. The higher your score, the better your opportunities to borrow. You'll also benefit from higher credit limits, lower interest rates, and possibly even more flexible terms and conditions.

Make it your personal challenge to improve your credit score, in the same way you would improve your physical health. Check in regularly so you know if there's anything wrong before it becomes a concern.

I promise you that learning to use these tools effectively will have a positive impact on creating more joyful finances for you and your family.

Remember, God is the greatest provider of all. He alone will ensure that you have everything you'll ever need. Credit cards can be very useful when used properly. However, if your motive for using them is fear that you need more than you already have, you may be displaying a lack of faith in His ability to provide.

4

The generous will prosper;
those who refresh others will themselves be refreshed.
(Proverbs 11:26, NLT)

If you're already familiar with my previous book, this chapter is going to be a refresher for you. You see, it's my opinion that in order to have joyful finances, you must be a generous giver. The Bible says, *"Be not deceived; God is not mocked: for whatsoever a man sows, that shall he also reap"* (Galatians 6:7, KJV). For the sake of your future finances, I want to encourage you to sow some seed money, and to keep in mind that every seed takes time to germinate. Plant today so you'll be able to reap as soon as possible.

As an aggressive reader in my twenties, I was introduced to Pastor Mike Murdock. Although he has authored many books, the one that undoubtedly changed my life is *31 Reasons People Do Not Receive Their Financial Harvest*.[5] This was a game-changer for me. I was very young when I read it the first time, and I've enjoyed rereading it several times since.

While there would be a benefit to me simply citing all thirty-one reasons he writes about in his book, for our purposes today we're going to explore just a few

---

[5] Mike Murdock, *31 Reasons People Do Not Receive Their Financial Harvest* (Fort Worth, TX: Deborah Murdock Johnson, The Wisdom Center, 1997).

of those principles that have helped me and my wife develop tremendous joy in our lives.

The Feeling of Giving

Even a child knows how good it feels to give something away. I'm reminded of an experience my spirited five-year-old had just two weeks before Christmas. Leading up to the holiday, he was thoroughly entrenched in the weekly retail flyers that seemed to find our kitchen table like mosquitoes drawn to water. I recall him flipping from page to page, saying, "I want Santa to bring me this" and "I want that for Christmas." If you knew no better, you would think this child had not a single toy of his own, or that he was seriously deprived.

That was certainly not the case.

After just a couple days of "I want… I want…" I simply couldn't take it anymore. It drove me nuts that my young children thought Christmas was only about the presents they would get.

An experience at their public school suddenly changed all this, rendering the weekly flyers nothing but a faded memory. The school had created a "Santa's workshop," and any parents who wished for their children to participate could send them to school with quarters and spare change that day to purchase used items that had been donated by the school's families. The organizers received all the items and displayed them on tables in the gymnasium, just like a real store, and the most expensive items cost no more than a dollar. All proceeds generated would be donated to the local food bank.

I'll never forget the excitement in my son's eyes when I returned home from work that afternoon.

"Daddy, Daddy!" he called, greeting me. "I can't wait until you see what I got you! Can we open our gifts tonight?"

For the next two weeks, he carried on.

"I think Daddy should open the first gift on Christmas morning, and it should be the one from me."

My son was experiencing something most people overlook or fail to allow themselves to experience. He was joyfully looking forward to Christmas morning not because of what he was going to get, but rather in anticipation of what he was going to give. His heart was filled with abundance as he waited for that blessed day to arrive.

There was a drastic change in him.

Throughout the following pages, we're going to walk through the joy that can come from giving, as well as how and when to give. Although it's not a science, there is an undeniable correlation between giving and receiving that cannot be overlooked if you wish to optimize the joy in your life.

What Does It Mean to Tithe?

At twenty-five years of age, if I were to be asked if I was a giver, my response, without hesitation, would have been, "Of course I am. I give $20 a week to my church, put a buck in the charity can at the mall every once in a while, and once a year I support a local fundraising group by purchasing a $35 coupon book that saves me hundreds of dollars in return. I'm not just a giver, I'm a smart giver."

Now, just to put this incredible generosity into perspective—and so you don't get the impression that I'm bragging about my unselfish heart toward money—I was a top-producing salesperson at the time with a very comfortable compensation plan. My annual earnings exceeded $100,000 and my annual expenses, including my home mortgage, car payments, taxes, etc., were less than $55,000.

When you add up my generous donations—$20 a week for the church, $35 for the coupon book, and maybe $10 for the times I shoved a buck or two into a charity can—you'd see that my annual giving equalled a little more than $1,000.

Hold the applause, please.

To the average middle-class twenty-five-year-old, this may very well seem like a significant contribution, but there was nothing average or middle class about my life. I was a single male with a car that was paid for by the company I worked for, and I only worked about twenty-five hours a week. With no children to support and both my parents healthy and independent, frankly I was out for myself. I didn't have a serious care in the world.

If my annual income exceeded $100,000 per year, and my total giving added up to about $1,000 annually, that means I really only gave one percent of what I'd been blessed with. One percent! I kept ninety-nine percent for myself.

Looked at another way, after my bills were paid and there were no more debts to cover, I had approximately $45,000 sitting in the bank, and I thought I was being generous by giving $1,000 to charity.

If I was being so generous, why didn't I feel fulfilled as a contributor to the great things happening in my community and beyond? Because I was holding back and not being obedient. When someone knocked at the door and led with, "Good evening, I'm canvassing to raise money for…" I'd immediately interrupt them and say, "I'm sorry, I can't help you. I direct my donations to my church." After closing the door, I would mumble something under my breath like, "Man, the nerve of that guy to come knocking at dinner time, trying to take my money..."

Does any of this sound familiar? Was I really the most selfish guy in the world? Truthfully, those people who knocked on my door were trying to support something they really had a heart for. Donating $5, $10, or even $100 to their causes likely would have had such a small impact on my life. But instead my immediate response was "Go bother someone else."

Does that sound like the heart of a generous and thankful person? I really was not acting in accordance with the blessings that had been given to me.

Would it surprise you to learn that by the time I was thirty-five, I was struggling financially? The pressure of new debts, financial obligations, and a shortfall in weekly cashflow often found me unsure of how the bills would be paid at the end of the week. In fact, just ten years after making more money than I could responsibly handle, I was drowning in debts so bad that I had to borrow money to make loan payments. Yup, you read that right: I had to take money from a line of credit to make the monthly payments on credit cards and building loans. How generous do you think my heart was at that very moment?

Then along came a reminder.

Just when I needed it most, I looked through the stacks of books in my living room. I've always been a reader more than a television watcher and my collection of personal development, financial planning, and business building books continues to grow even after twenty years of acquiring new reads.

Realizing I needed to make a change in my life, I sought out a special read. You know the kind I'm talking about—the book from which the words jump right off the page and hit you in the face, that book which you just can't put down because the author is speaking right to you.

I stared at one title in particular—the book by Mike Murdock about the reasons people don't receive their financial harvest. It had been a long time since I'd read it, and although I vaguely remembered it mentioning something about "give more, get more," I wasn't sure it was the right book for me. I really didn't have anything to give. I was in debt. Could giving help me with that?

One of my favourite sayings is "When the student is ready, the teacher will appear." I've heard this a lot over my years of business ownership and real estate investing. Blessed with various mentors in my life, they would remind me from time to time, "Ryan, when the student is ready, the teacher will appear." It was exactly what Mr. Miyagi would have said to Daniel LaRusso in *The Karate Kid*.

At various times in my life, I had heard about tithing. This lesson was one area in which I, as the student, needed to listen before I could really learn anything. An article on the website Ananda.org says,

> Tithing is a spiritual practice—just like prayer or meditation. It is the regular act of giving the "first fruits" of your labors to God.
>
> Tithing is an act of faith based on the divine principle that everything we have comes from God's hands.[6]

This may seem a little difficult for some to understand or accept. I get that. After all, you're the one putting in the crazy long hours and back-breaking work, right? If you're like I was, you're putting in those countless hours at night, too, only to find that your quality of life just isn't what you dreamt it being when you were growing up.

Within the sixty-six books of the Bible, the tithe is specifically mentioned in Leviticus, Numbers, Deuteronomy, and Malachi. But growing up, my Catholic Bible education consisted of only four authors: Matthew, Mark, Luke, and John. I had never been exposed to the other books and was nothing less than amazed to learn there were more than the four Gospel authors quoted each week at mass. I certainly received an education in respect to tithing.

Malachi 3:10 says,

> *Bring all the tithes into the storehouse so there will be enough food in my Temple. If you do," says the Lord of Heaven's Armies, "I will open the windows of heaven for you. I will pour out a blessing so great you won't have enough room to take it in! Try it! Put me to the test!* (NLT)

The life lesson provided by this short scripture is that if you observe the tithe, and give God ten percent of everything you earn, He will in return give you more blessings than you have room for.

How does that sound for increasing joy in your life? He will give you so much joy that you simply won't have room for it. Perhaps that's what your pastor meant at Sunday service when he suggested that we have overflowing joy.

---

[6] "The Purpose of Tithing," *Ananda*. Date of access: October 20, 2020 (https://www.ananda.org/the-purpose-of-tithing/).

Again, if you're like I was, you may not be receiving all of this information about tithing. However, isn't it wonderful that the scripture goes on to encourage us to test Him on this? It states this very clearly.

Well, I felt that this was my escape clause. It seemed easy enough to try.

In his book, Mike Murdock writes, "Your tithe is the Golden Gate to financial supply."[7] He further states, "The arrogant will not tithe."[8] When I read these two statements, I immediately thought to myself, *If tithing is the golden gate, then why in the world would I close it by being arrogant?*

To be clear, at the age of thirty-five, a point at which most of my friends were starting to earn significant incomes, drive nice cars, and take winter vacations, I was struggling to keep my head above water. Where do you think my joy level was during that time? It certainly wasn't overflowing, and there was plenty of room in my storehouse for more of it.

So my wife and I took the challenge. In very little time at all, we started to see an increase in joy in our household, in our business, and in our bank accounts.

Why Should You Give?

Biblical principles aside, we want to explore optimizing joy in our lives and how giving can contribute to this goal.

Possibly the most familiar holiday jingle at Christmas time is the one that declares, "It's the most wonderful time of the year." Is there a coincidence that we correlate a wonderful time of the year with a time when nearly everyone is consumed with giving presents to those they love and hold dear?

As a giver, I certainly know otherwise. For a giver, Christmas is a wonderful time because of the joy extracted from the giving that occurs. Whether a simple token to a coworker or a thoughtful homemade gift of personal value, or even a gift of kindness to a stranger in need, giving returns joy to the giver. In many cases, the giver may experience more joy from giving than the recipient experiences from receiving the gift.

If you aren't sure this is true, go ahead and test it. There's no underlying rule that says giving must be reserved for Christmas time. Take the next opportunity to give something to someone—and no, giving your cold to the rest of your family doesn't count.

Once the thrill of giving finds you, once you've had the feeling that comes from knowing you've had a positive impact on someone else's life, the concept of tithing will make more sense to you.

---

[7] Murdock, *31 Reasons People Do Not Receive Their Financial Harvest*, 138
[8] Ibid.

Imagine that someone approached you and said, "Give away ten percent of everything you have and you will be so happy." You would understandably think they were nuts. It wouldn't inspire you to change your giving habits, nor would it be likely to increase the joy in your life.

I want to encourage you to try out the following exercise.

1. Take an opportunity in the next twenty-four hours to give $1 to charity. You won't have to look too hard to find a cause. Nearly every big box retailer now asks if you wish to donate to a cause as you stand in the checkout line. Or you can find a charity box in a local coffee shop or in a rest station along a busy interstate.

2. In the next seven days, give $10 to a complete stranger. Find someone you have absolutely no relation to and simply give them the money, no strings attached. Will your life be changed for the worse by giving away this $10? If this effort prevents your family from putting groceries in the refrigerator, then these steps are all the more critical for you. If this step stretches you, I'm proud of you. Go for it. Find someone who needs that $10 more than you and release it.

3. Regardless of where you stand financially, I want to encourage you to prepare to give away a gift of $50 or more, to any person, organization, or cause you choose. The important thing here is not the $50 value. The point is to make a donation that is large enough for you to notice it. If making a $50 donation doesn't affect your weekly budget, I would encourage you to increase the amount to something that pushes you a little, something that challenges you to let go.

How do any of these steps relate to increasing the joy in your life? If we were honest about our current position in life, whether it be our health, endurance, or finances, we'd have to acknowledge that our condition wasn't arrived at overnight. For that reason, it would be foolish to believe that anyone who isn't a regular giver would suddenly become one. You have to start with baby steps.

So start small, but be intentional. When you give that first dollar, consider three things.

First, did giving that dollar change your financial position?

Second, how did you feel when that dollar was released from your hand? Did you experience even a second of gratification knowing that it would make a difference to someone?

And third, be acutely aware of how your donation gets returned to you. Pay particular attention to little things that happen to you in the days that follow. Does someone say something kind to you? Do you find a coveted parking spot right near the entrance of the store you visit? Sometimes we overlook the little things that pack a punch in terms of joy.

One of the most challenging aspects of giving is that people flat-out love money. And when you live in a state of insecurity, whether with your job, your relationship, or your money, you're constantly afraid of letting go because you fear it will never come back. You only gain freedom in these areas when you understand that in letting go you're opening a door for joy to come back to you even stronger than before.

There's an old saying that says, "If you love someone or something, let it go." It's often quoted in terms of relationships—typically during the rocky times when one person leaves. The remaining person comes to realize that if their other half doesn't return, there really wasn't much relationship there in the first place. But if they do return, it's likely that the relationship will last forever.

You may thinking right now, *But I don't love money.* And I would like to believe you, and if that's true then you're already on your way to joyful finances because you know that in releasing the money you have you are opening a door for more and better things to be returned.

> We're so insecure in our relationship with money that we tend to believe if we give it away, we may never get it back—or we may not have enough left over.

A lot of people I know, myself included for the first forty years of my life, make large sacrifices every day in order to acquire more money. We're so insecure in our relationship with money that we tend to believe if we give it away, we may never get it back—or we may not have enough left over. This generally leads to hoarding and stockpiling, but in the end it's evidence that we're really living in fear and lack. We want to move beyond that way of living.

As you proceed through steps two and three of today's exercise, intentionally pay additional attention to what goes on around you and in your life thereafter. If the principle of tithing really works, and I firmly believe it does, then I expect the joy in your life to increase in direct proportion to the degree that you're willing to commit to it. I can't wait to hear about how your life begins to change.

Perhaps as you're reading this, you're thinking to yourself, *But I don't belong to a church right now.* Or maybe *I don't go to the one I do belong to, so where can I give?* One of the most difficult yet important lessons my wife and I learned from our experience is that there is no right or wrong place to give. We used to absorb ourselves in studying all the charitable organizations in search of the perfect one. We used to think that a cause had to qualify in order to be good enough to receive our support. We certainly don't wish to just throw money in the trash, so some wisdom is required of course, but the reality is that God isn't concerned about where you sow your tithe. He's only interested in seeing you exercise your giving heart.

Let's say you see a homeless person on the street. I used to think that if I gave him $5, he would likely just use it to get drunk or high. Inevitably, I would create a justification for passing him by without giving him even a quarter.

When my wife and I first looked at sponsoring a child through a global organization, I remember thinking, *Oh yeah, they take your $40 a month and only $4 actually gets to the child. I'm not giving $36 just so the organization can have a bunch of rich executives!* That's just another excuse not to give.

Isn't it true that any organization has to have administrative costs? No one can work for free. While I might not agree with a non-profit executive earning millions of dollars a year, the work those organizations do nonetheless changes lives for the better. Because of the work they do, infants are protected from fatal disease, children are fed, and adults are educated to become productive.

If our focus is on the wrong thing, it's easy to discount the importance of giving.

Sow on Fertile Ground

Take some time to consider the fact that if you haven't been giving, you haven't been receiving either. There's no way to determine exactly how much joy you've been robbing yourself of, since the joy that's returned is in proportion to what you give.

No one starts getting into shape by running a marathon the first day. If you aren't a long-distance runner to begin with, you have to start by taking a two- or three-kilometre jog, and over time, perhaps a lot of time, you can build up to the full 42.2-kilometre marathon.

I remember the early days of my own marathon training. I was struggling to finish five-kilometre runs, all the while wondering how in the world I would ever complete more than eight of these bad boys in a row. The answer revealed itself as I continued to practice every day of the eighteen-week training plan. The program was run by Hal Higdon, a very accomplished marathon runner, so it was simple for him to break down the keys to successfully training for a marathon if someone had never done it before.

I truly hope you can use this book to increase the joy in your life in a way you've never before dreamt possible.

When you decide it's time to get started, one of the key factors is consistency. Some people will give $100 to an incredible cause like curing cancer. Perhaps they buy a ticket for a dream home and consider that a donation. They have little to no expectation of winning, but they think this charitable act should win them some brownie points in heaven.

Aside from the fact that buying lottery tickets is nothing short of gambling, there are two additional reasons such contributions may not yield joy.[9]

The first reason may seem a little contradictory at first glance. When you give, you need to do it with no strings attached, but you also have to expect that it will be returned to you tenfold.

"That doesn't make sense," you may say. "Isn't expecting something in return exactly what 'strings attached' means?"

Not for a giving heart. When you give with your heart, you're giving with absolutely no expectation. If you learn of someone in need of a medical procedure and you decide to gift them $50 toward their need, it's crucial that you not expect a dime in return from this person. A giver knows that they have sown into someone's life, and for that they will be blessed in another area of their life. The benefit they receive will most probably come from a completely unrelated source. So when you give, have a full expectation that you'll receive ten times the blessing you provide; have no expectations, however, from the recipient of your gift.

Just to be clear, this principle applies to organizations just as much as it does to individuals. There can be no exclusion. We need to refrain from limiting our hearts with thoughts such as *I would give to this charitable organization, but I don't think they manage their money well so I'm going to pass.* That thinking only limits the blessing you will receive in return. Those thoughts steal joy from your life, and possibly other people too. Don't let negative analysis steal your joy. Give with no expectation of the recipient and full expectation of increased joy in return.

The second reason that supporting a charitable lottery may not garnish the kind of joy you're expecting is due to inconsistency. Givers are givers all the time. They are, therefore, blessed all the time. Of course it's wonderful to support your nephew's entrepreneurial start-up, but if that's the only blessing you've provided someone this year, it may not lead to constant and sustainable joy in return.

---

[9] Of course there has to be a winner. And yes, one out of every thousand tickets wins something. But that's not the kind of joyful return we can rely on.

This is where tithing comes in. One of the secrets of tithing most believers fail to understand has to do with consistency. If I asked who has a more generous heart, a person who writes a cheque for $1,000 or a person who gives $20 every week of the year, who would you think it is? An accountant may compare the annual figures and conclude that the totals are nearly the same, that both givers are equally generous. He would be correct. They are generous to a similar degree, but which of them has a more giving heart?

Have you ever gone on vacation to a resort? The type of resort I'm thinking of is a big place with swimming pools and restaurants, a spa, a fitness facility, and all kinds of sports courts. Perhaps there's even a golf course! All these amenities are spread out over hundreds of acres. The backdrop is the ocean, and the property is lined with trails for walking or jogging.

Ambitiously, you rise early on the first day of your stay to start something you've been wanting to do for a long time: jog. The scenery is beautiful, you have no conflicts in your schedule, and if you fall down halfway through, oh well. At least no one knows you. It's perfect.

By seven-thirty in the morning on that first day, you've covered the five-kilometre path through the woods, passing by the outdoor gym in which other ambitious vacationers are already working up a sweat. You did it! You gave it your all and you felt the pain, but you pushed on and now you're ready to start your day with some muscle-soaking.

While you were hitting the trails, you passed someone who has been running for years. They start every morning with a two-kilometre run regardless of where they are. For them, it's a quick pick-me-up. They've adopted it as part of their morning routine, no different than some people have a cup of joe. They've been doing it so long that it takes very little effort. Their body is used to it. Upon their return, they're in and out of the shower, dressed, shaven, fed, and on their way to the rest of their day in the same amount of time it takes you to bend down low enough to untie your shoes.

Do you see how important consistency is? The power of fitness certainly doesn't come from being an Ironman one day a year—an effort which, for the record, may require the rest of the year to recover from. It comes from consistently taking positive actions that benefit your body.

The same is true when we prepare ourselves to be givers and receivers of blessings.

Remember the exercise I mentioned earlier in the chapter? Those three steps were designed to get you started on the path to becoming a giver. They were small steps, to plant seeds in your life that you can expect to harvest down the road.

To finish this section of the book, and to set you on a path that will most certainly increase the joyfulness in your life, I want you to commit to repeating those three steps every month for a year.

"Test me on this," says the Lord Almighty. Do this with a complete expectation that your life will see abundant increase in your joy and you won't be disappointed at the end of the year.

Remember, however, that running five kilometres on your first day of vacation makes you no more a seasoned runner than making a single $1,000 donation makes you a seasoned giver. Consistency is the key.

Find a way to tithe. Work your way up to it. Keep in mind that practice makes everything easier. Even the tortoise understood that a consistent effort would get him to the goal line. He just needed to stay the course.

Don't worry about what others may think. Don't compare your abilities to them. Just give selflessly, consistently, and have the full expectation that you'll soon reap everything you've sown. Just as a farmer faithfully tends to the field of seed he has planted in the springtime, you too will reap a harvest to fill your storehouse in the fall.

PART

Who Is On Your Side?

TWO

5

Beware of false prophets who come disguised as
harmless sheep but are really vicious wolves.
(Matthew 7:15, NLT)

As a child, I loved to watch, draw, and play G.I. Joe every chance I was given. I had no concept of what war really is or what it would take to lead an army into battle, but make no mistake about it: everyone must learn these vital skills at some point in their lives. If we don't, we stand a high risk of being devastated by the perils of combat in our day-to-day lives.

The battlefield I'm referring to is in your own local community. It's a financial war, and every day people become casualties of the never-ending fight. The enemy is everyone who wants you to surrender to them. Every time you turn on your TV, you're under attack. Each time you scan the internet or walk into your favourite store, the war is on.

Are you confident that you're winning the battle? Have you ever even considered that there's a battle going on? If not, think again!

In this financial war, the media is a giant attack force which offers a platform on which to do battle. Billions of media dollars are spent annually in an effort to defeat you.

In this war, it was once explained to me that each dollar you earn, receive, inherit, win, or otherwise come into possession of is a soldier in your personal army against poverty. Did you ever dream of being poor when you were a child? Waking up with anticipation that one day you might owe more than you could possibly afford to pay back, or not have enough food to feed your family? Did you consider ending up homeless and living on the streets? Of course not. People don't dream of having nothing.

So why do so many have so little? The answer is that they didn't build, nurture, and protect an army that could in turn grow and fight on their behalf.

Think about it: what does your current army look like? If you think you're a one-man army, then I'm afraid you are easy prey for the professional snipers on the other side of the line. Very few people, if any, are well trained enough to fight and win the war singlehandedly.

When this concept of building an army was first presented to me, I immediately thought of all my G.I. Joe heroes. Each figurine I owned had a specialty: a tactical fighter, a sharpshooter, a knife thrower, a fire specialist, etc. They all worked together because, depending on the circumstances they found themselves in, certain skills were more helpful than others.

I'd like to walk you through an exercise that's going to first identify for you the kind of war you are waging. It's hard to win a fight you haven't realized you're in.

Ask yourself the following questions, recognizing that every one of us is in the middle of some kind of battle, and that the answers will vary based on individual circumstance. If you discover that you're losing the battle right now, know that you're certainly not alone. The good news is that once you identify the war, you can train up your soldiers in order to reclaim your battlefield and claim the victory you've been promised.

1. What percentage of your household income is spent on necessities? This includes water, food, shelter, and clothing.
2. What percentage of it is invested?
3. How much consumer debt do you have? This includes car loans, furniture loans, lines of credit, student loans, etc.
4. What percentage of your household income do you spend on eating out and/or entertaining?
5. What percentage of your household income do you donate, tithe, or otherwise give away?

By identifying where significant percentages of your money are directed, you can identify what kind of attack you're under.

For example, if the above questions revealed that forty percent of your income goes toward necessities, zero percent is invested, forty percent covers your debt, twenty percent takes care of your entertainment costs (with the balance being charged to credit cards), and zero percent is consistently given away, your battle becomes clearer.

Perhaps you read those hypothetical figures and think to yourself, *How does he know where my money is going?* The answer is, I don't. These percentages are simply representative of what people have shared with me. Whether young or old, people's situations have a general consistency. Why?

Well, there's something else to consider as you look at each of those five questions: when you put money in those various places, who benefits?

Understanding the Opposition

People often think that their employer is trying to take advantage of them, despite the fact that they're paid for the hours they work at a predetermined rate. When a person's paycheque fails to meet their spending habits, the employee often turns their back on their employer for failing to pay enough for the employee to enjoy the life they feel that they deserve.

What would make the employee feel this way? Didn't they agree in advance to trade a week's worth of work for a mutually agreed upon rate of compensation? Of course they did, but then the war began. On one side you have a hard-working person while on the other side stands the relentless world of marketing and consumerism. When the hard worker comes home from a long day at the office, they turn on the radio, internet, or television—and what do they hear?

Let's have another look at those five questions.

Do they read, watch, or hear anything about ensuring that their family has the basic necessities of life? For example, maybe a toilet paper commercial comes on. The company is claiming their toilet paper is softer and thicker than their competitor's.

How often do they read, watch, or hear information regarding investing? Again, a few types of commercials come to mind, but they are few and far between, and generally the commercials are designed to sell a financial institution; they're not designed to inform you of the importance or benefits of investing.

How much of what we read, watch, and hear outside our workday is related to a business selling consumer products? It could be as high as seventy-five percent of everything we take in. Perhaps the reality is even higher than that.

Think about this for a moment. Big box stores advertise their goods 24/7 on every form of media you have access to. Car dealerships always seem to have the deal of a lifetime and can get anyone approved today. Furniture stores hold a "sale of the year" every weekend.

You can't escape it. Everywhere you look, you'll find someone trying to sell you something. They're trying to convince you that their product is a must-have if you want to be happy. How can you say no?

Well, unless you figure out how to say no, their side wins the war.

I can share from personal experience that I used to think I was placed on this planet to become the best consumer out there. I was a huge target for sellers. I once agreed to purchase a $5,000 parking lot and within hours got sucked into paying an invoice for more than $18,000 for a job that was a complete scam. The money was gone, the product didn't make me happy, and that's the moment I realized I was in a war and not on the winning side.

Have you ever considered that spending so much money on entertainment and eating out can be an attack on your finances? Not likely. After all, the commercial said, "Treat yourself. You deserve it!" You work hard and give your best all week long, so who could argue that you don't deserve that sizzlin' sirloin with a loaded baked potato, honey buns on the side, and a crisp salad to kick things off? Now, don't forget the sixteen-ounce beverage of your choice, and if you order one appetizer, you get the second one for fifty percent off.

Go all out, it's Friday! Your friends have driven across town to join you. This is the place where you meet at the end of a crazy week to compare battle stories.

So you proudly say to the waitress, "This round's on me!" Everyone around your table cheers in gratitude for your generosity.

Then it hits you, and you remember that you're not carrying cash.

No problem, you think to yourself. *I'll charge it and pay it off as soon as the bill comes in.*

All the while, the war is still raging. The restaurant has created a tremendously successful battlefield. They've placed you in an environment that allows you to quickly justify each and every expense. When you leave the establishment with a full belly, your pockets are empty.

Of course, not every night is like that. Thank goodness for fast food restaurants that allow us to work extra hours without having to worry about preparing, eating, and cleaning up a sensible and healthy meal at home. Instead we pull up to a drive-thru window and have just about any meal we want, handed to us almost instantly without even needing to leave our car.

Chalk up another victory for the other side.

Lastly, how often do you read, watch, or hear anything regarding the benefits of charitable giving? Perhaps this happens during the holidays. Maybe you're told to give to the local soup kitchen or food bank to help others enjoy the holidays, too. After all, no one should go hungry at Christmas time.

But what's in it for you? What's the advantage of giving or tithing? If you never read, watch, or hear anything about the power of generosity, how can it be expected that you would budget any portion of your income toward it? For this reason, the average person gives away so little that the percentage is close enough to zero that the giver is unable to reap any noticeable reward.

Protecting and Growing Your Army

I want to tell you a little story about Jack and Joan, and the experience they had as seasoned business owners, trained financial professionals, and disciplined people.

Despite everything Jack and Joan had learned about investing money, such as keeping it out of reach and ensuring it's protected, they still learned a costly lesson. As a result of a series of transactions, they found themselves in possession of a significant sum of cash. They had dreams about using it to upgrade their yard, but until the day came to spend it they decided to store it in a safe place.

There was a problem. Although the money was safe from outsiders, it was far from safe from them. Just like everyone else, they were waging a war against consumerism.

Sadly, when other spending opportunities came their way, the stole from the stash, promising to replace it as soon as possible.

Then, as it always does, tax season rolled around, and they had a pretty steep balance to cover.

"No problem," Jack said confidently. "I'll just go deposit some of the cash and we'll pay the taxes right away and move on."

Let's face it: the government always gets theirs, so there was no point delaying the payment.

Then, about two months later, they got an unexpected invoice from their accountant that added up to more than $10,000. The accountant claimed that because of all the complex transactions they had reported that year, he had to invest a lot of extra time sorting everything out.

After the irritation subsided, Jack calmly returned to the stash, made another deposit at the bank, and proceeded to pay the accountant.

You can see where this is going, right? Those two expenses alone ate up nearly $25,000 of what they'd thought was a huge stack of money.

Feeling angry about having to give away so much of their hard-earned money, Jack made a rash decision. He wanted to spend some of the money on himself and Joan. They had young children at the time, and they'd had visions of using some of the money to create a more joyful life for their family.

But the war was heating up, and soon they were attacked from yet another angle—from the world of recreational boating. Having grown up on the water, this was a weakness of Jack's. He justified to himself that a boat was exactly what the family needed.

> You can't ever let your guard down. Your finances are always under attack, and if you think having more money is going to change that, you're dead wrong.

You can't ever let your guard down. Your finances are always under attack, and if you think having more money is going to change that, you're dead wrong. It only gets worse when other people think you have more money for them to attack.

Back to the boat. Jack was surfing the internet one night, browsing mindlessly. Suddenly, there it was: a deck boat. This type of boat has all the furnishings of a fancy pontoon boat, but it's as fast as a speedboat. It was perfect. Finally, he would get to spend some of that stash on his family!

"Honey, we need to go see this boat tomorrow," he said to his wife. "Now, hear me out. The kids are young, and if we had this boat it would be so great to take them tubing, skiing, and fishing. We could even take nice rides up the shoreline in it. It's going to be so great!"

With no chance of winning the fight, Joan joined Jack on a visit to the dealership. And inside of a week, another huge chunk of their cash was gone.

After this purchase, there was nearly nothing left. In fact, by the time spring rolled around and they returned to their conversations about upgrading the yard, as they'd initially intended, there wasn't even enough money to pour the concrete pad they had envisioned.

Damn! Jack said to himself. *I let my guard down, got caught up in the excitement of having access to all that cash, and then I fell victim to marketing. It won this battle, hands down.*

He felt like an idiot—like a victim, really—but he was the one who had made the decisions to spend the money rather than properly save it. Because he'd failed to protect his soldiers, they were taken to the battlefield and slaughtered. It was as if his dollars showed up on the beaches of Normandy, completely unprepared and fully exposed to the ambush awaiting them.

The purpose of this story is to demonstrate that despite one's education, ability to earn money, and experience with investing, we can all fall prey to this constant battle being waged against our finances.

When this happens to me and Megan, we've learned that rather than feeling victimized, we need to look at the experience like a lesson. The lesson here is to ensure that our money is stored in a place that keeps it safe from strangers, and keeps it safe from ourselves as well.

More money is not the solution to most people's financial struggles. Understanding the war and protecting their soldiers is.

6

Good planning and hard work lead to prosperity,
but hasty shortcuts lead to poverty.
(Proverbs 21:5, NLT)

When getting started, having so few soldiers to work with means having little power in your army. Think of your savings account as an army base. This is where you train and multiply your troops before sending them into battle. Once a strong base has been established, we can look at what to invest in.

This chapter will discuss various ideas related to saving. We want to create a healthy breeding ground for our soldiers where they can strengthen in numbers. We must formulate and execute a plan to achieve this over a realistic period of time.

"Should I keep a stash in my mattress?" you may be wondering. While I think you might sleep better at night if you had a mattress full of money, that's not exactly what I have in mind. Neither is a shoebox or a hole in the ceiling tiles.

My first suggestion is that saving needs to be automatic. Start by speaking to your bank about how to have ten percent automatically taken off your paycheque before you even see it. Some online banks, such as Tangerine.ca, will allow you to set up automatic withdrawals in minutes. If you haven't tried anything like this before, I would encourage you to set up an account that isn't as readily available as cash in a shoebox. Remember Jack and Joan from the last chapter? That's a good reminder of why you'd want to store the money remotely.

To Save, Invest, or Donate?

The important thing is that you need to start saving, investing, and donating a portion of your income on a regular basis. In the beginning, actually doing the actions of saving, investing, and donating is more important than how much you save.

> ...actually doing the actions of saving, investing, and donating is more important than how much you save.

While most people are well-intentioned when it comes to these three areas, they may not be aware of the war they're in. So many people are losing this battle because they always seem to think their current circumstances need to change before they can make their first move. Here's a valuable tip: your finances won't change on their own. If you wish to win the war, you can't just play defence. You have to set up an offence and begin your own attack.

To change your financial habits, consider dividing your income in a new way. First and foremost, financial gurus everywhere consistently suggest taking ten percent of your income and immediately saving it. This is a great starting point. As you become more experienced and disciplined, you may decide fifteen to twenty percent is even better.

Whatever percentage you decide to save, an equal percentage should go towards tithing, charitable donations, and investing.

The rest of your income—which is a majority—will likely be directed toward covering your cost of living.

It's a good idea to take money off the top for these other purposes. And when done this way, most families stop noticing the missing money after a fairly short period of time. In the event that you still doubt your ability to make ends meet after automatically withdrawing these percentages, it may be wise to review your lifestyle more thoroughly and determine whether the path you're on leads toward joy. It's possible you're stuck in a losing battle right now that's dragging you down.

The weekly budget we discussed previously will provide tremendous insight into where the money you make actually ends up. Often the solution to financial shortages is not to bring in more money, but to become more aware of how it leaves. Until you're made aware of this, it's difficult to understand how to make the most effective changes.

For instance, you may not realize there's a problem with grabbing a quick lunch each day because you consistently make healthy choices in what you eat. When you review the spreadsheet, however, you'll realize that the budget isn't very healthy. Your weekly lunch expense is adding up to nearly $100. By spending $20 at the grocery store and taking the time to do some meal planning in the morning, that expense could be reduced by eighty percent!

That's the kind of smart money management that can lead to a better use of your resources. It would help you find the ten percent you need to save, which you might have thought was impossible before.

Where Should You Send Your Soldiers?

We've already established the importance of automatically transferring your savings out of your income every month. The reason is that it eliminates the impact of your emotions from the process.

But where will this money go after it's taken out of your paycheque? For most investors, there are only a few options, and they are generally selected by using two main criteria. First, how involved do you want to be? And second, how comfortable are you managing risk?

Understanding your level of interest and ability to monitor, manage, and manoeuvre your savings is very important. By its very definition, the word *savings* refers to funds that get set aside for future use. This means they aren't used to pay off the credit card next month or make a bulk payment against a loan balance. Nor are they used to finance your annual family vacation. Those expenses should have their own account.

Your savings could be considered to be part of your soldier family, which you plan on nurturing and growing. For the sake of this discussion, let's assume you start by putting aside $100 per month. You set up a system to take it off your paycheque before you even see it. Well, where does it go then?

Here are just a few suggestions to get you thinking.

1. Send your money to an isolated savings account at the bank. This won't generate much interest, but we aren't necessarily focused on using this money as an investment. We just want to begin the habit of saving, separately and automatically. If you decide to move this money to a separate bank account, make it an account that requires two signatures to withdraw funds. This will eliminate the temptation to quickly borrow from your savings to pay an incidental bill.

2. Put the money in a tax-free savings account (TFSA). These savings tools are relatively new in terms of public awareness. They're government-regulated savings accounts that offer a little more return while still providing the comfort of a safe environment. Each year, you're permitted to contribute a regulated amount of money to this kind of savings account. The maximum permissible amount is determined by previous contributions. Once funds are directed to this account, the owner still has immediate access to them, so this isn't considered a long-term investment vehicle. It's simply a savings tool.

3. If you want to lock up this money a little tighter, you can ask your bank to direct the funds into a GIC (government-issued certificate). These are essentially loans you make to the government. They offer small returns, usually less than two or three percent, but are considered extremely low-risk. Some might suggest they are investments, but since the return will struggle to keep up with inflation I see it as a savings option. GICs generally require a short-term commitment, such as a one- to three-year term. During that time, your money is locked and protected. One strategy may be to purchase a new GIC every six months, so that at some point in the future you'll have this money maturing at regular intervals. This requires a little more time and energy than simply transferring the money to a separate savings account.

4. In the event that you're a little more of a risktaker, but you lack the time necessary to become an educated investor, another strategy could be to approach a financial institution and ask what kind of savings tool they could provide if you directed a predetermined sum to them each week or month. This isn't an investment tool, either, but it's a relatively low-risk way to put some money away for a rainy day, or for a much greater cause in the future.

To be certain, the savings a person generates in their twenties, thirties, and forties may look a little different, and have an alternative motive behind it, than those saving in the second half of their lives. Before you reach fifty, your main objective may be to strengthen and increase the number of soldiers in your army so they stand the best chance later in life. Save, build, deploy! Save, build, deploy!

In time, as you succeed on the battlefield, your emphasis may turn away from deployment and more toward saving. In order to establish a comfortable base for your soldiers to retire, it's critical that they go out and win some battles so they can grow in numbers and strength.

We can think of our money like a giant ocean freighter. Did you know that the safest place for those huge ships during a storm is at sea, not in the harbour? They're prone to take more damage when they're parked in a harbour during a storm, so it's safer for them to be on the open seas, navigated by a skilled captain amidst the tall waves.

Similarly, if you just park your money and hope it will weather the storms of your thirty or forty years of working, you may just find that it sank somewhere along the way and you failed to notice. For many, the only way to recover from a disaster like this is to seek government handouts or continue working until the day they die. Don't let that be you. There's nothing joyful about that.

Let's start today. Gather the troops and get excited about the future.

Once you've established a strong base from which to work, you can begin to deploy your soldiers. The golden rule here is that time waits for no one, and the earlier you start, the better your chances of success will be.

7

Deploying Your Troops

He cared for them with a true heart and led them
with skillful hands.
(Psalm 78:72, NLT)

With a base camp of soldiers ready to enter the battle, safety and protection must always be at the forefront of a good leader's mind. As the steward of your platoon, you must consider your options, calculate your risks, and evaluate the benefit versus the cost at all times.

When considering the greater good, from time to time you will have to sacrifice one for the survival of many. In terms of your investments, sometimes it's necessary to consider an expense, or a loss, as the cost of doing battle.

For instance, it may be necessary to pay a transaction fee—such as one percent of the value of the transaction. However, if by completing that transaction your platoon grows by ten percent, you can quickly justify it.

The design of this chapter is to share my investment walk with you. I'll introduce you to some investment ideas, but it's not possible to list all the vehicles you have to choose from. I hope this chapter will encourage you to consider investing in a way you never have before. By the end of it, hopefully you have a crystal-clear understanding of the difference between saving and investing. And with any luck, you may even re-evaluate how you're managing your troops so they can begin a new mission to better serve you and your family.

Early on in my financial career, at age sixteen and having recently acquired my driver's license, I started a lucrative summertime business: Evernew Lawn Care. Having no money management experience or knowledge, I did what ninety-nine percent of children do: I asked my parents for advice, because in my mind they still knew everything.

Good information about how to manage one's finances wasn't mainstream and the school curriculum didn't offer any level of training to prepare students to lead their troops after graduation. Therefore, the people who understood the world of finance were generally university graduates who specialized in the subject. Perhaps by the time you read this book, our school boards will have recognized the need to better equip young people to flourish in the real world as opposed to just surviving in it.

In fairness to teachers, however, how can they be expected to teach what they don't know? It would be very difficult for them to share anything more than their own experience with money. My experience has led me to believe that there is little to no experience among those who are in charge of teaching our children. So if you were holding out for a handsome inheritance from an aging family member, don't hold your breath.

Two Steps

1. Set the goal. Let's get back to the analogy of our personalized army. If you were planning to release your troops into battle, you would clearly relay to the troops the goal. You can only expect to get the best out of every soldier if they understand and get behind the mission. Before sending them out, both the leadership and the foot soldiers should be on the same page.

So set your goal before the troops leave your base. Understand very clearly what you wish to accomplish. This is how you'll know if your mission is successful.

Additionally, understand how much you're willing to sacrifice before retreating if your plan doesn't work. In the event that you lose a quarter of your platoon, are you willing to stay in the fight, or is it time to retreat and re-evaluate? Perhaps you're willing to wager fifty percent of your investment, or possibly only ten? Know what winning and losing looks like before heading into battle so you can direct your soldiers confidently. No one wants to serve a leader who's shooting at a moving target, nor will they rally behind someone who doesn't know the difference between victory and defeat.

It's much wiser to pull out of a battle and re-strategize once in a while than to sacrifice your entire army and be forced to start over because you couldn't admit you were losing and take necessary action.

2. Lean on experience. So I turned to my parents with a shoebox of hard-earned lawn care money and asked, "Okay, what do I do with this?"

There wasn't a moment's hesitation.

"We'll set up an appointment for you to meet our financial advisor," my father responded with pride.

He had a good reason to be proud. As a skilled trades labourer, working for a major car manufacturer, my dad made a very good middle-class income. Rather than trusting his own instincts or just squirrelling the funds away in fear, he and my mom had taken a faithful step and entrusted their money to someone who studied the financial industry.

As we arrived for our introductory meeting, I read the advisor's name on the big sign above their office. Walking in, we were greeted by a friendly woman who kindly asked us to take a seat while she let Mr. Trustme know we had arrived.

Within minutes, Mr. Trustme welcomed us into his boardroom by way of a long hallway lined with framed certifications, degrees, and diplomas, explaining where all the extra letters behind his name came from. The meeting room consisted of impressive presentation materials and it had a refreshment bar. This man sure had my attention. He appeared to ooze success. Clearly this must be a good place to leave my money.

When he spoke to us about future plans, long-term gains, market stability, investment diversification, and tax planning, his words seemed riddled with wisdom. I was captivated. As a young businessperson and investor, I would come to turn over tens of thousands of hard-earned dollars to Mr. Trustme and his team.

Years later, we would learn that the entire show was little more than smoke and mirrors. His fancy catchphrases were designed to persuade us to believe he cared more about our long-term financial growth than he did his own. His primary goal had been to convince clients to turn over their money to him so he could buy paper stocks and reap the commissions for doing so.

His plan was tremendously successful—for him and his family. They lived in big houses and drove fancy cars. Mr. Trustme even owned his own airplane.

But what about his clients?

This proved to be a critical lesson. You should understand that no one cares more about your financial health than you do.

> You should understand that no one cares more about your financial health than you do.

Several years after advising my parents that they could afford to retire early based on the financial foundation they had amassed during their working years, Mr. Trustme called them in one day for a very serious meeting. I insisted on joining. My interest in learning about finances had me so curious about everything.

This meeting would reveal the true nature of Mr. Trustme and his organization. He began by advising my parents that they had about eight years' worth of financial resources remaining, so perhaps they should consider getting a part-time job. Then he proceeded to suggest that they sell the family home, which they had built and paid for thirty years prior. And although my father had retired so he could follow his passion for fishing, he recommended that they sell his boat, since boating was very expensive. The icing on the cake was his suggestion that owning two vehicles wasn't necessary, now that they no longer worked, and that selling one of them would make sense.

My blood was boiling as I listened to this financial forecast.

Mr. Trustme decided this would be a good time to inject a positive perspective into the meeting, so he reminded my parents that they were approaching the age of sixty-five. Based on how little money they had, at least as far as he figured, he encouraged them to try qualifying for an old age benefit from the government which would potentially bring in $6,000 per year.

Understand that this wasn't a lot of money, even back then. It was a slap in the face. And with his gold rings covering three of five knuckles, he decided to share with my parents that he himself had just reached that same golden age.

"Would you believe that the government won't give me that money, because we make too much?" he said.

That was it. I couldn't take it anymore.

I stood up in total disbelief and threatened to punch this crook right in the jaw. My parents had to restrain me, and then we decided it was a good time to leave.

That man had lost nearly their entire life savings and created a mountainous debt they would be responsible to pay back… and now his advice was to sell what they had left and give it to him so he could do… what? Pocket it also?

Know When to Retreat

Thankfully, I was in my twenties when this lesson presented itself. Clearly we were losing the battle, and much of the platoon had been slaughtered. But we took immediate action to save the remaining troops and get them back to a safe place where they could grow in strength again.

Together, my parents and I formulated a personal investment plan. As I'm sure you can imagine, such a devastating blow can take a long time to recover from, so we took our time, planning and preparing to go back into battle with a much different angle of attack.

What I took away from our years of experience with Mr. Trustme was that if you simply turn your money over so someone else can use it, you're exposing your troops to abuse and neglect that's sure to crush your army and leave you wondering where all your soldiers have fled. You have to make it your responsibility to understand what's being done with your money, how it's being done, where it's being done, for how long it will be tied up, and at what point it can be turned back over to you with its increased power and potential.

This book isn't solely dedicated to explaining individual investments, so we won't analyze them. However, when you approach a financial advisor, you may consider buying a paper asset. Paper assets include a stock, bond, mutual fund, registered retirement saving plan, insurance, etc. These are the type of products most financial planners have access to. With the money you turn over, your advisor will have the ability to purchase a piece of paper that indicates you are the owner of a specific number of stocks in a particular investment.

You may give him $200 at the end of the week, with which he'll make a purchase. Next month, you'll receive a statement that shows your purchase and ownership of these mutual funds, for example, and it may even show that your investment's balance has grown to $204 in paper value. Way to go! You made a $200 investment, and the value increased before the statement even got to you. Does it get better than that?

Perhaps you hit the jackpot on this one. You think to yourself that your advisor is the best advisor in the industry. Who wouldn't? And so you start giving him your weekly investment with new aspirations and dreams for the future, anxious to see that next statement.

Let's fast-forward six or seven years. Your statement arrives and, to your amazement, you've nestled away a nice $40,000 paper balance. The market has gone up and down, you're told, but because your advisor has "diversified" your money, you're protected from the volatility of it all.

You decide that you'd like to consider some other investment options, so you call your good advisor friend and have a conversation.

"Hi Joe," you greet him. "I've been thinking about investing in a business idea and I'd like to use my $40,000 as seed money. Can you please write me a cheque next week for the full balance? I'm going to close the account."

"Oh, do you really think that's a good idea?" he says. "You've worked so hard to save these funds for the long-term. The numbers prove that your portfolio is growing. Through compounding interest, the growth has just begun."

Joe does his best to persuade you not to withdraw his income—I mean, your investment.

"But you see, I've been operating my own small restaurant for years," you explain. "My parents are friends with the owners of a fast food chain and they're willing to give me the first franchise restaurant in our area. This is too good of an opportunity to pass up. I happen to need $40,000 in order to purchase the franchise."

"Gee, that does sound like a great opportunity. Let me see what I can come up with."

Excited that your paper asset balance happens to be the exact amount needed to buy into this wonderful investment opportunity, you call Joe back the next day.

"Hi Joe, can you please confirm when my cheque will be ready?" you ask.

"Well, the administration is calculating your balance for you and…"

Before Joe can continue, you're impatiently beginning to question the delay. "My balance is $40,112. I'm looking at the statement right now."

"It's not exactly that easy. You see, the balance on your account is subject to fees, penalties, taxes, and a pat-on-the-butt charge, so it takes a little while to figure out exactly how much of that is actually yours…"

Getting irritated and running out of patience, you simply instruct Joe to have a cheque available for pickup by the end of the week, at which time you'll come by to receive it.

Let's step outside this example for a moment. What kind of feelings and thoughts are running through your head at this point? Well, to begin with, you're finding out that money goes into your advisor's hand a lot easier than it comes out. It certainly hadn't taken a week for them to figure out whether they would take your money. In fact, if you had wanted to increase your monthly contribution to $300, a simple phone call and about five minutes would have done it, no further questions asked.

But what about all these new terms, such as *penalties, fees,* and *taxes*? Is this the proper time for you to learn about the exit clauses? Of course not. Going into any investment, a good investor should know their exit strategy. Right at the start, you need to ask, "What will it cost to get out when I'm done?"

Back to the story.

When Friday finally arrives, you're thinking about what you'll do after you get the money. The franchise sales representative had explained that once they picked up the $40,000 cheque, you can attend training school and get the ball rolling on your own new restaurant. It's all planned out. You can see the future building, the sign, and the parking lot full of satisfied customers.

Wow, this is really happening, you think. *I'm making my dreams come true!*

As 9:05 a.m. arrives and your financial advisor's office opens for the day, you step up to the front desk to collect the cheque that will be used to set your future in motion. You've worked hard for the last six years to make your monthly contributions regardless of personal circumstance, and now it's time to really move things forward.

You see the envelope with your name on it is sitting on the edge of the counter. Excitement bubbles from your fingers as you quickly greet the receptionist, offer some ID, and snatch the cheque before bouncing back to your car.

Once inside, you tear the top off the envelope to confirm that all your dreams are about to come true. Wrestling with the paper to get the cheque out, your fingers work faster than you can manage. You're finally able to pull the cheque free to admire the…

"Wait. What?" you say. "This has to be some kind of a mistake. Where is the rest of my money?"

In total disbelief, you're staring at a cheque made out for $17,892.41. You thought you were picking up a cheque for $40,000… the $40,000 you need to purchase a restaurant franchise.

Exiting your car with more than bubbles inside you now, you march right back to the front desk and demand to see your financial advisor.

"Where is my money?" you demand. "I had "$40,000. I need $40,000. What the heck am I going to do with less than $18,000?"

With flashes of your franchise dream going up in smoke, your face as red as flames, you're learning about the importance of having an exit strategy—a part of the process that wasn't clearly understood at the beginning of the investment plan.

While this example may sound extreme, the very same situation has played itself out for two different people I know. I expect it happens more often than most people want to believe. A discovery like this one is devastating!

Here's the lesson: have an exit strategy before you start. Understand what success looks like and know what you have to do to reach it. Then have a plan for how to proceed when you do.

Let's look at another example. You decide to invest, and you start with monthly contributions of $100. Great job! The amount isn't important, but starting the process absolutely is. Your advisor suggests buying 1HappyDay stocks each month and expects that by the time you retire, which is thirty to thirty-five years down the road, you'll have a healthy nest egg.

Does that sound like sound financial advice?

Truthfully, if you bury $100 every month in your backyard for thirty-five years, you'll have a decent nest egg also, so what's the difference?

Every salesperson—I mean, financial advisor—will certainly tell you about the eighth wonder of the world. There are only seven, you thought? Oh no, make no mistake about it, the eighth is clearly *compound interest*. This beautiful concept is the idea of your soldiers having babies, who in turn have babies, who in turn have even more babies. Eventually, the first soldier you started with becomes an army.

The longer the babies keep having babies, the stronger your platoon is going to grow. So the key to capitalizing on compound interest is to start as early as possible.

Now, a hole in your backyard is not the most attractive place for your troops to be having babies. The advisor is correct: it is important to get your money into the market as early as possible. There is a place for these types of professionals in your investment plan.

With an understanding of why and how to start investing, our focus needs to turn to why, when, and how to stop. To decide this, you can't rely on advisors, because the decision to pull out your money, quite frankly, will mean a reduction in their own income. Of course this isn't their favourite part of the process.

For you, however, the exit strategy is when you actually get your money back, using the army you've built to pay for your lifestyle. So you need to discuss the financial implications related to applicable income taxes, penalties, and other institutional fees that may be associated with withdrawing your money.

Here's an important word of caution: don't trust your advisor to provide you accounting guidance regarding tax planning. They simply aren't qualified or knowledgeable enough in this area, regardless of how much experience they may claim to have.

Right from the start of your investment process, seek a professional accountant and advise them of what you're attempting to achieve. Provide them an outline of the plan your advisor has given you and ask them to provide guidance on what will happen in thirty to thirty-five years when you're looking to withdraw a certain amount each month to live off.

Bear in mind that the accountant may not understand the institutional fees charged by the advisor, or the specific penalties that will be associated with the withdrawals, which is why it's critical to employ the services of both professionals, the financial advisor and the accountant. Together they should be able to provide you with a financial plan that matches the level of risk you're comfortable taking.

This is the beginning of building a successful team. At this point you will have a banker, a financial advisor, and an accountant working with you to set up and execute your financial future plan. As you grow and develop, you will have opportunities to add other professionals in fields such as law, insurance, mortgage financing, the stock market, and the real estate market. It may take time to develop relationships with professionals in each of these industries, but as you do, the potential of your plan will continue to expand.

Your plan must be simple enough for you to understand it from start to finish. If you don't understand what's being done with your money, how long it will be held, when you will begin to get it back, and how much the plan will cost to execute, remember that someone is simply trying to sell you something. You need to ask more questions. If you keep asking questions and they don't provide clear answers, run. Take your money and find a different set of advisors.

It may sound like too much work. But this is your financial future we're talking about here. Isn't it worth the work?

Not all advisors are created equally, so don't feel compelled to trust the first one you meet. Understand that it's a business like any other, and just like any other profession, there are good business operators… and there are others. Don't just blindly trust your financial future to someone who doesn't deserve to be trusted.

This has been a pretty heavy chapter, so let's see if we can wrap it all up before moving on to examine the various types of investments you may wish to consider.

- First, it's critical to start the process of investing immediately. Immediately! Not "as soon as possible," because there are always reasons to put it off just a little longer.
- You need to build a team. You'll start with your banker, a financial advisor, and an accountant. With a plan in place, in time you may expand your team to include other professionals, such as a lawyer, an insurance broker, a mortgage broker, a stock broker, and even a realtor.

- Collectively, your team will build a plan with you based on your available resources, your level of risk comfort, your end goal, and your timeframes. This plan will include how to get into the market, how much you will invest consistently, how long you will be investing, how much it will cost you along the way, when you will begin withdrawing from your funds, and the financial implications of doing so.

When you have a financial vision for your future, and a group of people committed to assisting you to achieve that future, it will become clearer that joyful finances really can be a reality for you.

Next we're going to look at some entry-level investments that you can direct your army toward.

8

Pick Your Battles

The master was full of praise. "Well done, my good and faithful servant. You have been faithful in handling this small amount, so now I will give you many more responsibilities. Let's celebrate together!"
(Matthew 25:21, NLT)

Today, there are limitless opportunities for investment. In this chapter, I want to stir your imagination to see opportunities you may otherwise overlook.

You may not think you have enough money to start the process, but before you allow your thoughts to drift in that direction, I want to share a quick story I recently heard about a young man named Bill.

Bill was disappointed with how his life had gone thus far. He was thirty-eight years old, had been working his nine-to-five job faithfully for more than fifteen years, and felt that he had little to show for his commitment, even though he loved his wife and two children. His mortgage seemed like it would never go away, he was hoping his car would outlast its payment plan, and there was never enough money for the family to take a vacation. As for retirement savings, he just shrugged his shoulders and said, "Yeah, sure. I'll win the lottery before I retire."

That all changed one day as Bill was sitting on his lunchbox waiting for the buzzer to alert him back to his desk. While sitting there, he overheard someone complaining that his car had broken down and needed $500 to fix. This guy was tired of making repairs and had decided to give the darn thing away and buy something reliable.

If I can come up with the $500 to fix the car and get it tuned up, maybe I could flip the thing and make a little extra money, Bill thought to himself.

Bill asked his fellow employee if he would consider giving him the car so he could try fixing it. That was the encouragement the car owner needed to make the decision to replace it once and for all.

He got the car repaired in no time flat, pulling together all the money he could to buy replacement parts, and included a little TLC to make the car look like it was ready for a car lot.

About seven days after ownership, Bill sold it to someone who was very pleased to pay $1,500.

Bill immediately went online and found another car that needed some work, and he reinvested the $1,000 profit. Within two weeks, he had turned his $500 into more than $2,000—and thus began a used car dealership.

Fast-forward five years and Bill had become a very successful businessman with a thriving dealership and service business. He and his family now enjoy annual vacations to beach and ski destinations and he's begun to save for that coveted retirement day.

Bill changed his future with $500 and an idea.

The point to this story, which I have experienced time and time again in my own career, is that the times when you have the least amount of money are also the times when you're forced to employ your creative genius. Yup, I said it. You are a genius! We all have genius within us, but only some capitalize on the talents they've been given. Most fail to recognize those talents even exist, making it unlikely that they'll prosper.

So how will you capitalize on your talents?

I will say this: if you would rather give your money to someone else to invest because you don't like the risk associated with gambling, you may be better off just sticking it in a shoebox. Expecting that someone else will care for your finances more than you will is just that, gambling. Sure, there are some good and honest advisors out there, and if you find one they may make you some money, but whether they make you money or not, remember that they have bills to pay. Even when your funds aren't doing that well, they still have to put food on their table and a roof over their head. Where do you think that money comes from?

Whether you have $500 to start or $50,000, make investment choices that are consistent with the level of risk you're willing to take. Dozens of resources online teach people about how to measure their risk tolerance when evaluating investments. The purpose of risk tolerance tests is to determine whether you're a conservative, moderate, or aggressive risk-taking investor.[10]

Wealthy investors repeatedly say with confidence that it doesn't take money to make money, because they know that the first investment a person makes is themself. If you just visit a public library, speak to a professional in the industry, or surf the web for related educational materials, you'll begin to see an immediate return on your first investment, before you even spend a dime. Where's the risk in that?

How much should you invest in yourself before you're ready to make real investments? That's a loaded question.

Imagine that a good personal improvement course costs $5,000. Well, some people might think that if they spend all their money on a course, they won't have anything left to invest in the market afterward. That very thinking will have led them to only have $5,000 in the first place. Until that kind of limited thinking is corrected, it would be wise to continue investing in yourself before you risk your life savings in a world you aren't familiar with.

The amount to be invested is going to be different depending on the person. It's similar to leading a troop of soldiers into battle. How many soldiers would feel confident if their leader was selling ice cream from a truck yesterday and today is in charge of strategically leading four hundred men onto the beaches of Normandy? An extreme example, perhaps, but the point is clear. The better you prepare yourself to be an investor, the better an investor you will be, period.

To assist investors in setting up boundaries on when and how much to trade or invest, a friend of mine, Bryan Burke, has developed some guidelines which he calls "trading rules." With his permission, I have listed the top three here, but you can find the rest on his website.

1. Trade with the Trend—You can't change the weather, but you can set your sails to take advantage of whichever direction the market wind is blowing.
2. Stick with a Trading Method You Have Confidence In—Realize you don't have to be right on every trade. A few losers doesn't mean your trading system is defective.

---

[10] To increase your knowledge of investment terminology while simultaneously learning about your own risk tolerance, visit the site of my friend and mentor Bryan Burke, at www.academyofti.org. Bryan's company offers investors of all levels an opportunity to learn and develop new strategies for trading and investing, offering one-on-one personalized coaching as well. One of the resources Bryan's team makes available is a risk tolerance test, and I would strongly recommend that everyone take a test of this nature before investing.

3. Measure Your Results—You're trading to make a profit. If your figures don't add up, stop putting money at risk until you know why your stock trading method isn't working.[11]

Buying Your Staples

Every time my wife and I go to the grocery store, we default to a standard list: eggs, milk, bread, etc. From time to time, we'll go out of our way to visit a specialty store to acquire items we might not find at the traditional grocery store.

Investments work exactly the same way. Most people go to the general investment store and shop for the standard items everyone else buys, but be aware that there are specialty stores out there that offer a vast variety of investment opportunities you might not find while shopping at your favourite bank or broker's office.

I'll refer to the basic items—mutual funds, retirement savings plans, stocks, and bonds—as the staples of investing. Let's take a quick look at each of them and discover why they're so popular.

Mutual funds. Mutual funds are pools of money collected from multiple investors. Rather than having to purchase a company yourself, using millions of dollars, a professional money manager combines smaller value investments from their client base in order to purchase stocks, bonds, or other assets that individual investors would otherwise be unable to afford on their own. Each party in the mutual fund then receives a percentage share of any returns or profits from the security in relation to the amount they invested.

There is a general perception that your money could be safer in an environment such as this for four main reasons.

First, the cost to own mutual funds is minimal. For instance, there are some mutual funds with no minimums. However, most mutual funds require a minimum initial investment of anywhere from $500 to $3,000. Of course, there are other funds that require much more than that, but a mutual fund is a flexible upfront buy-in opportunity. It does appeal to most investors.

The second reason is that you're not alone. Isn't it a lot more comfortable to do what everyone else is doing rather than feel like you're the only one giving it a go? A mutual fund collects funds from multiple investors, and with their combined contributions they can leverage their power to make things happen. Most investors like the feeling that others are with them, and hope that there truly is strength in numbers, as the saying goes.

---

[11] For the full list, visit Bryan Burke's website: www.academyofti.org.

The third reason is that a mutual fund is a collection of assets that are pooled into a portfolio. If you were to invest in one, it could consist of assets such as stocks, bonds, and real estate—and even some businesses as well. The safety net is that even if one sector of the market should decline, you'll still be okay because the real estate or business investment may still increase in value. This is called diversification, and in my opinion it's an overused word to provide investors with a false sense of security.

The fourth reason that a lot of investors opt to purchase mutual funds is that they're being sold by someone they know and trust: the professional money manager. The money manager's job is to convince investors to give up their hard-earned money, so relationships are vital in this industry. Once the investor turns over their money, the manager becomes responsible for buying and selling investment tools that will achieve the investor's goals. Personally, I cannot imagine the pressure that must come with having to meet the expectations of hundreds of investors, many of whom have put forward their life savings.

Take the example of Donald. From a very young age, he was encouraged to purchase mutual funds. His parents didn't know much about how to invest, so the best advice they thought they could give him was, "Go see our financial guy, Ted. He'll get you set up with mutual funds. They're safe, inexpensive, and you don't have to do anything. Ted does it all."

As a nineteen-year-old student with aspirations of a solid retirement, Donald takes his parents' advice and gives his money to someone who is one step away from being a total stranger, learns little to nothing about what his money is actually doing for him, and is expected to trust that in forty years or so, Ted—and whoever replaces Ted when he decides to move on—will manage his money well enough that the net gains will support the future Donald has envisioned for himself.

Does this sound familiar? There can be no doubt why the average person is broke by the time they turn sixty-five years old in Canada. Too few people are teaching young people to raise up their own financial army by way of education and hands-on experience. The middle-class investor is so busy working hard to earn money that they don't have any time left over to invest. They don't take the time to learn about it, and their fear of losing everything they've worked so hard for is crippling—and that same busyness prevents them from getting the kind of returns they would really love to get.

Surely you've stood near the watercooler and listened to someone brag about how they got a double-digit return on their investments last year.

Gee, I'd like to get a double-digit return, you think to yourself. *But seriously, who has time to figure out how to do that?*

After all, you have a guy. It's his job to do the best he can to make your money grow. If he can't get double-digit returns, why in the world would you think you could? You're not a professional money manager.

A word of caution: always remember that money managers don't work for free. Whether or not they're successful at growing your money, there is a fee associated with their service. Your investment may experience double-digit growth for decades, but your actual account balance may only increase five to eight percent in the best of years. Often, money managers take their cut off the top, to make it less obvious to the investor. Regulations are now in place that require managers to disclose their fees directly, but to the uneducated investor who has little time and less energy to direct toward the issue, it can easily be overlooked.

Registered retirement savings plans (RRSPs). While most people consider getting an RRSP, by its very own name it is only a little more valuable than stuffing your money into a mattress. I'll explain why in a moment.

The most significant benefit to this type of investment is that it's made with *pre-taxed* dollars, and the interest earned is compounded without being subjected to capital gains taxes, income taxes, etc. The value of the funds are only taxed at the time of withdrawal, a time at which the investor is expected to be retired and earning less money. Thus the perception is that the tax bracket in which they will qualify would be less than if they were to withdraw the funds during their working years.

Here's an example. If you invested $100 toward your RRSP today, you may qualify for a $40 tax credit that year. The tax credit would vary based on your current tax bracket—and since the more you make, the higher you are taxed, the more you are taxed, the more beneficial this refund will appear.

Most advisors assume that you'll earn less money once you retire, so the appeal of this type of investment is that when you withdraw the funds, you'll be in a lower tax bracket. Perhaps you withdraw the funds while in a thirty percent tax bracket, for instance, meaning that the tax associated with the funds becomes ten percent less than if you would have withdrawn them twenty years prior, at the height of your career.

Sounds good, right? It sounded really good to Sandy also. So good, in fact, that Sandy considered taking a $50,000 personal loan so she could top up her missed contributions from prior years. Yes, these investments are so good that the government only allows you to invest so much in them each year. Should you invest more than the permissible percentage of your annual income, you could face heavy penalties. So be sure to know what you are permitted to invest.

RRSPs hadn't been on Sandy's investment radar for a long time, so with no prior contributions to include, she didn't have anything to be concerned about.

She started doing some basic math. If she borrowed $50,000 and made a top-up investment in her RRSPs, given her current forty percent tax bracket, she would get a refund of $20,000 almost immediately. She could apply that against the $50,000 loan and really only have a loan of $30,000 outstanding.

At this point, most wide-eyed money managers would be trying to convince you that you just earned a forty percent return on your investment, and most investors would quickly agree. I do not. See, in order to not have to pay back the $20,000 refund, Sandy won't be allowed to touch her $50,000 investment. Because if she does, guess what? The government will want to tax it.

There are a couple of exceptions to this, whereby the investor can withdraw the funds for specific purchases, but the funds must be replaced in a specific period of time, otherwise the value is taxed.

Sandy considered that she was twenty years away from retirement anyhow, so if she invested the $50,000 at a modest six percent annual return, her computer calculators suggested she would have more than $160,000 saved up in her RRSP when it matured.

How's that for a return? She borrowed the money, made the investment, and then ended up with three times the amount she'd started with some twenty years down the road. It's simple to see why this strategy is such an easy sell, wouldn't you agree? And every single day, millions of investors buy into mathematical speculations just like these.

Well, my scepticism forced me to analyze these calculations a little further. Here are the things I started thinking about.

Sure, the $20,000 immediate refund was awesome, and it reduced an otherwise $50,000 loan to just $30,000, if applied to the loan immediately and in full. From personal experience, I know that suddenly having access to $20,000 can bring with it much temptation. Why not use it to pay off the high-interest credit card balance first, or update that clunker in the driveway you've been talking about replacing for two years? Why not just take a one-week vacation? Heck, you've been working so hard lately… you deserve it!

The little red angel on your shoulder will be whispering a whole lot of encouragement to do things you otherwise would know aren't good ideas.

Suddenly, Sandy could find that she only has $15,000 to apply against the loan. And she might even be able to justify and feel good about her decisions.

Regardless of whether Sandy ends up applying the full amount, she still has a real-life loan to deal with.

"Consider it a forced savings plan, not a loan payment," her money manager may remind her. "After all, you have $50,000 worth of RRSPs now, and you only have to pay for $30,000 of them."

Taking his good reasoning into account, she could adjust her monthly budget to ensure she is able to meet her new $521.94 per month loan payment for the next six years, when the loan will finally be retired. She's just injected into her budget the equivalent of a new car payment. Do you think she was expecting that? Of course not. But sales is sales, and she's just been sold.

Money managers are going to read this and argue that the $50,000 investment will grow tax-free and compound during that six-year period, and for another fourteen years thereafter, without Sandy having to invest another dime. So really, when you consider the total investment of $35,000, inclusive of the original loan and interest, that's a great way for Sandy to have invested her money.

Compared against a scenario where she invested nothing at all, I absolutely agree.

But now we need to have a look at what the investment might really be worth when Sandy is prepared to withdraw her money. If the $50,000 was invested at an annual interest rate of six percent for a total of twenty years—before taxes, fees, and any form of penalties that may be applicable—Sandy would have a balance in her account of a little more than $160,000! That's amazing, right?

At first glance, that may be the case. But allow me explain why it may not be as great as it appears.

First off, whenever I hear a money manager propose an RRSP, they are assuming that the investor will be making less money when they retire than while they're working. That should be your first warning, really. Isn't retirement supposed to be about living the good life? If you're struggling to afford travel and doing the things you like during your working years, what kind of retirement plan would suggest that you'll be making less money once you quit your job? Should the plan not be to invest so that, at minimum, you make the same amount of money later but have more time to do the things you want?

Ever since I was twenty, I've realized that I want my income to be higher when I retire. For that matter, it better still be growing in order to keep up with the increasing cost of living. Why in the world would I invest for forty years in a plan that assumes I'll have less income when I stop working? That's limited thinking, if you ask me.

In the event that Sandy's income does go down when she retires and she starts withdrawing her investment to supplement the shortfall, she's still going to be taxed on this income. Perhaps it will only be at thirty percent rather than forty percent, but regardless, this would mean that one-third of her investment will be paid to the government. Sandy's new total will be closer to $105,000—if it's withdrawn slowly. If she were to take it all at one time, the injection of income would actually *increase* her tax bracket.

Do you see the point here? Regardless of when you pay the government, you will pay them. Sure, there may or may not be tax savings available through an RRSP, but by no means is it so significant that it makes these vehicles the sort of low-risk, high-return investments everyone should have.

Here's another great question to ask: what happens to your RRSP if you die? Likely your spouse or children would inherit the value of your RRSP, which would be wonderful, but at what cost? Well, let's say you had $50,000 at the time of your passing. The $50,000 inheritance would be added to the recipient's income that year and taxed as though it were personal income, likely at the highest tax rate possible. In most cases, the government, although saddened by your loss, will happily take fifty percent or more of your RRSP balance before your heir can even think about what just happened.

Another way to approach these figures is to look at the actual gain. Historically, we have witnessed the value of currency double in value every ten years or so. This means that the cost of living does about the same.

If Sandy puts $50,000 away in 2020 in the hopes that she will retire in 2040, how well will her investment keep up with the increasing value of currency? $50,000 in 2020 should be worth $100,000 in 2030, and by 2040 it would need to be worth nearly $200,000 to have the same purchasing power.

Let's put it another way. If Sandy has $50,000 to purchase a car in 2020, by 2030 that same amount of money would likely only buy her a vehicle worth about $25,000 in 2020. By the time 2040 rolls around, that same $50,000 would only afford her a vehicle worth about $12,500. The point to be made here is that when money managers try to project the value of an investment several decades down the road, they use figures that appeal to the investor in today's market, often overlooking the actual value that the investment will have in the future market.

To wrap up my thoughts regarding RRSPs, of course any investment is better than no investment, so if you're totally stuck and have no idea how to invest your money but know you really have to start doing something, then RRSPs are a very inexpensive way to begin your journey. It's not difficult to open an RRSP yourself online or at your local bank, and money managers everywhere are available to initiate these kinds of investments for you.

However, be reminded that these are savings plans designed to help you park your money, not necessarily *grow* your money. The risk of losing your investment in this type of vehicle is very low, and thus the returns are reflective of that risk and are also very low. They may be a great tool to help you achieve goals such as saving for an education or buying/building a home, but they are very limited in their ability to create any significant growth.

Tax-free savings accounts (TFSAs). By their very name, it's clear that TFSAs allow you to save after-tax dollars, growing them along the way, without further taxation penalties thereafter. Since government always gets their cut first, the popular thinking is that it's better to give them what they want before you invest your money rather than after.

Different schools of thought come into play here, but the important thing to know about a TFSA is that if you invest $50,000 and it grows to $70,000 over time, you own all of it. There will be no taxation penalty upon withdrawal because the invested money had been taxed beforehand.

Regulations are in place to limit the annual contribution one can make into such an account. However, the unused contribution room from years gone by can be made up for later.

Should you decide to withdraw the money for personal use, however, then you cannot replenish the funds unless there's still an adequate allowance based on your contribution limits. In the unfortunate event that you over-contribute, you can expect a government-imposed penalty of one percent to be assessed to your account balance.

In my opinion, this is a good way to park and add soldiers to your army. It's a savings vehicle, however, not an investment tool. Returns vary, and the owner of the funds must be actively involved.

My suggestion remains that the best investment a person can make is in themself. Learning how to protect and grow your soldiers personally is both a non-taxable investment and will serve you for your entire investing career.

Stocks and bonds. Enter the world of legalized gambling. What's the difference between speculating on the future value of a specific stock and betting whether the ball is going to land on a black or red square? The sad reality is that both gambles can change in an instant. Regardless of how much research you do in advance of taking your position, only a few people in the world have the power to influence the outcome. In other words, you have no control over the outcome. You put your money on the table and pray like heck that it will still be there when you're ready to leave the game.

I realize this may appear a tad pessimistic, so I'll illustrate the point with a personal experience. I remember the thrill of once watching a man—we'll call him Roger—try to beat the casino.

Roger appeared to have solved the roulette wheel, or at least he thought he had. For hours, he methodically placed bets, kept track of the numbers, and strategically changed the value of his bets based on his wins and losses. His formula was reasonably simple and seems to replicate the thinking of many money managers.

Roger's approach was to identify a streak whereby the roulette ball landed on a number of the same colour many times in a row. Depending on what he observed, he would either try to ride the streak or bet against the tide.

I enjoyed watching Roger's patience as he waited for a streak of four or five black numbers in a row. Using deduction, he justified that each time a black number came up, the law of averages suggested a greater percentage that the next number would be red. Seems like solid reasoning, right? Roger would initially place a small bet on red, starting with the table minimum of $10. If he won, he would continue betting $10 in hopes that a streak of red would turn his $10 into $20, and then $40, and so on; each time he won, he would just take $10 off the top and let the balance ride. When he lost, he returned to betting the minimum amount and began the process over again.

Admittedly, this was pretty impressive. I watched as he took his initial $100 and turned it into more than $1,800 in just a couple of hours. Roger was a college student, and certainly no one was willing to hire him for $900 per hour, so he was feeling pretty good about his newfound source of income.

And then it happened. With five red numbers in a row already on the board, Roger decided to bet $25 that the next number would be black.

It was red.

Roger quickly put $50 on black and waited for the ball to find its groove.

"23 red is a winner," the dealer announced.

"No worries," Roger said as he reached into his pocket and placed a $100 bet on black again. He figured he had lost $75, so if he won $100 now, he would cover his losses and still be ahead $25.

There now appeared a flaw in his reasoning, despite his strategy having served him well so far.

The streak of red continued, and before I could figure out the odds of this happening, the ball had landed on five more red numbers in a row. Roger had kept upping his bet to compensate for the losses, and soon he was out of cash. He now made his first run to the automatic bank machine between spins, withdrawing enough money to cover the $1,600 bet that followed.

"Double zero is the winner," announced the dealer to the table.

Inside of fifteen minutes, I watched Roger lose everything he had won as well as the extra money he'd pulled out of the bank machine.

I felt a little bad for the guy, really. The ball had suddenly seemed to be drawn to red numbers like a magnet. He lost $3,000. As my shoulders sagged for this young gambler, I figured he had learned a valuable lesson. I grabbed my drink from the waitress and began walking away.

Then a bit of a commotion around the table caught my attention. Roger had gone back to the bank machine and withdrawn his maximum daily limit—in desperation. He proceeded to place a $1,685 bet on black.

The entire room waited in silence as the ball rolled, bounced, and slowly settled into its new resting spot.

You could have heard a pin drop. No one dared to say a word. All eyes bounced between Roger, the table, the dealer, and then back to Roger.

Another person sitting at the table suddenly celebrated. "Yes! Red again!"

And it was over. Roger had lost his entire college tuition gambling on what had seemed to be sure odds. He had no control over the outcome, despite all the data having suggested that he should expect a favourable outcome.

I had to stay and watch what would happen once Roger removed himself from the game. Would you believe that the little roulette ball found sixteen red numbers in a row before it landed back on a black one? Unbelievable!

Now, how is this anything like investing in the stock market? That's a great question. The comparison is so similar that it has permanently tainted my perspective on this form of investing. Take this as a disclaimer: while some people make lots of money doing it, I have learned, like Roger, that too many uncontrollable variables affect the outcome.

> ...the first, most profitable investment you will ever make is in yourself.

Let me repeat this fundamental truth: the first, most profitable investment you will ever make is in yourself. Before entering the stock market in any capacity, you need to invest a little in some education. Reading this book is a great start, although it hasn't been designed to teach you strategies that will help you beat the markets. If you plan to invest in the stock market, you owe it to yourself to learn about the companies you may wish to invest in. You most certainly want to ensure that you understand your own current financial position, know what you want to achieve, and decide how much you're willing to lose. Having these parameters in place before you start will take a lot of the pressure off. Knowing your personal limits is a healthy place to start.

Also know how much it costs to play. When Roger sat down at the roulette table, he knew the minimum bet—and that if he placed his money in the right place at the right time, he would receive a predetermined amount of money.

In my opinion, this is one way in which gambling is actually more transparent than investing in the markets with a professional manager.

Let me recount a conversation between a woman named Marie and her money manager, Kent. It went something like this.

"Hi Kent," Marie says. "I just received my monthly statement in the mail and had a chance to review it. I have a couple questions. Do you have a moment?"

"Of course, Marie. What can I help you with?"

"Well, I see that last quarter my management fees on the account were $2,417. Can you please tell me how much money I've actually made during that time?"

Kent clears his throat before responding. "Sure. You see, that's a difficult question to answer because I'd have to crunch some numbers first—"

"But Kent, I can see exactly how much I paid you, and yet I can't see how much my investment is worth," she says with some irritation. "Did the value of the investment at least increase by $4,834, so that we essentially split the proceeds?"

He tries to put her at ease by deferring her question and avoiding a factual response. "It doesn't work like that, Marie. You have to look at the bigger picture and stay in the game for the long haul. By the time you retire, we expect that you're going to have a nice cushion to draw from. It's a twenty- to twenty-five-year outlook."

Sadly, this kind of conversation happens every day between managers and clients. Managers are quick to forecast results. They always take their fee, though, and when the tough questions are asked the situation becomes very grey.

This sort of scenario has driven a record number of self-trading investors into the marketplace. Today, with the use of simple online tools,[12] someone can purchase or sell any volume of shares within minutes, at a single fixed cost of less

---

[12] There are many resources available, but two common ones are Wealthsimple.com and Robinhood. com.

than $10—and for as little as zero dollars. If you only have $20 to get started, in many cases you can buy $20 in the company of your choice. And just like that, you're in the market.

While no one can legally predict the future value of a stock, the cost to buy, sell, and hold should be precisely calculated and transparently explained. When purchasing, you want to know what the transaction fee is. You also want to know how much it will cost to sell. But if you decide to purchase and hold for a while, you should also be advised of exactly what the "management fees" are. This is generally a percentage of the balance in your holding account. Be sure that you're clear on what your costs are, inclusive of all fees, so that you're very much capable of determining your breakeven point, how much you're willing to lose on a particular investment, and what the sell triggers are.

There's another reason that investing in the stock market is a lot like gambling: the influential power of only a few affects the value of all. What Roger didn't realize is that his game had certain influences that affected the result, influences he had no control over. For instance, it's possible that the wheel he was playing on was slightly tilted, or that there was a groove in the wood. Or, much more plausible, perhaps the dealer could control, to a certain degree, where that ball was going to land. In any event, there was absolutely nothing Roger could do once he was invested to increase his odds of success.

The same truths apply when you purchase a stock. Only a couple of people in the world are influential enough that their buying and selling can affect the entire market. Everyone else in the world is essentially powerless.

For example, if you purchase Tim Hortons stock today, your stock won't be affected if you go out and buy more of their coffee. The stock's performance is dependent on the actions and decisions of owners, CEOs, and board members you will never meet. All the while you hold onto your piece of paper and hope that you bought at the right time and that you'll sell before the wrong thing happens.

It looks a bit like our casino example, doesn't it?

Start Small

Of course, there are professionals who make each of these types of investments day in and day out. They're both educated and experienced in their field, and thus they expose themselves to considerably less risk than the rest of us.

Regardless of which style of investment you choose, I would strongly encourage you to start small—as small as possible.

I'm reminded of one of my closest friends, Andy, who's an incredibly smart guy. He became the first person in his family to successfully complete postsecondary education, graduating with a law degree. Andy is always eager to learn something new.

Recently, Andy shared with me his newfound interest in stock trading. He had figured out how to create his own account on Questrade.com within minutes and quickly learned that there was a nominal fixed cost per trade. He was making two or three trades a week.

The most significant part of his story is that after doing this for a couple months, he still had only a little more than $300 invested. Andy knew from firsthand experience that no matter what you decide to do in life, there's going to be a learning curve—and a cost. Unlike with his law degree, which had required a five-figure loan, learning about the stock market only required a few hundred bucks, and he could take his time to learn at his own pace, free from high-pressure salespeople.

I'll contrast Andy's story with something I heard from my aunt and uncle, one of my favourite couples in the entire world. They're tremendously hardworking and have done very well for themselves.

In the early stages of their marriage, my aunt and uncle decided to get involved in a rental property investment. My uncle was amazingly handy and my aunt was one of the kindest and most social people in their city, so together they knew they would make a dynamic investment team.

It really did seem like they would be great landlords, but they failed to account for their lack of education in both property management and social studies. Including the cost of financing, a ten percent down-payment, land transfer taxes, legal fees, and a small investment in making the property ready for rent, they ended up wagering a very large amount of their hard-earned money.

Their ambitions were quickly squashed when not only did their tenants fail to make the rent payments, but when they vacated they left behind a property in need of thousands of dollars of repairs.

They learned a lot of lessons through this experience. More than twenty years after this experience, I still can't discuss with them opportunities to partner on real estate investments, because they make it clear through their tone of voice and facial expressions how stung they still feel from their negative experience.

My heart goes out to anyone who works hard and tries to make good decisions only to have their dreams stomped on.

The purpose of sharing these two stories is to encourage you to take some action today, despite how scared you might be, but do it in an affordable fashion. This way, when you make a mistake—and notice that I said *when*, not *if*—the cost of that mistake won't hurt you financially enough to knock you out of the game or taint your perspective on future investments.

To wrap up this chapter, I want you to remember that each dollar you earn, inherit, or are given is a soldier in your army. It's your responsibility to protect them to the best of your ability.

Although we've touched on several potential battlefields, my strongest advice is that you know as much about your opponent as possible before committing too much artillery, otherwise your opponent will have the upper hand straight out of the gate.

While the information I've shared in this chapter may have introduced you to some new ideas, however, realize that it is by no means an all-inclusive list of what you should understand before making a financial investment. Starting is the most important step, but I caution you to start slow and take baby steps, since you will make mistakes along the way. When you're beginning, you'll fare better if your mistakes are small and less expensive to weather.

And if you've learned nothing else from this chapter, be sure to read this next sentence twice: have an exit strategy in place. It can be very expensive to make a whole bunch of money on paper, only to find out that you'll lose half of it when you try to put that money in your pocket. Know when you're going to leave the battlefield, and what conditions will trigger that exit. Know how much it is going to cost to leave.

Next, we're going to have a look at how you can win on the battlefield of business.

9

Formal education will make you a living; self education
will make you a fortune.
—Jim Rohn

As we continue forward, we're going to change gears a bit. This next chapter
is dedicated to sharing some of the experiences Megan and I have enjoyed
in business over the last three decades. Business may offer some of the most
powerful benefits in terms of strengthening your army and having a big impact
on the battlefield. What you're about to read are real life experiences that all came
with a silver lining.

Know first that memories are merely thoughts, not necessarily a factual
account of what really happened. As Megan read through the chapter you're
about to read, her recollection of how things happened turned out to be much
different than my own.

We've had many discussions about our business experiences over the years,
which in and of itself is among the greatest benefits of being in business—the fact
that she and I have done it together. At the beginning of our relationship, she was
working for an accounting firm. We then decided that it would be much better if
she joined me on the battlefield. And so our journey together began.

I think the best definition for the word business, although there are many, is this one: "the organized efforts and activities of individuals to produce and sell goods and services for profit."[13]

Perhaps you read the last chapter and, like me, you think of yourself as more of a hands-on investor. You know about paper assets, and you've done some homework to educate yourself on how to buy low and sell high, but two things have always eluded your investment strategy: first, you've never had financial capital of any significance to invest, and second, time has never been on your side. So you work hard to support your family and there just doesn't seem to be enough money left over at the end of the day to really get anything going. The idea of learning how to invest seems like too much a time commitment.

You may have even considered quitting your job, which would free you up to build a business. But what would you do to earn income while your new venture takes off?

Until I read a book called *Cashflow Quadrant* by Robert Kiyosaki, an American businessman and author, I always thought that being self-employed was the same thing as being a business owner. That book was quite a revelation, however, in terms of clarifying the distinction between the two.

During the first half of my business career, I did groundskeeping, landscaping, 3D design, multilevel marketing, residential and commercial cleaning, and real estate holding. In the second half, with a better understanding of leverage and equipped with Kiyosaki's teachings, my wife and I changed strategies. We got involved in business start-ups and acquisitions, including a property management franchise, an inflatable rental business, a privately owned government agency, a building maintenance company, and an outdoor power equipment sales and service business.

In short, I went from being self-employed to owning businesses. So what *is* the distinction between the two?

Kiyosaki explains that a self-employed person is responsible for nearly every aspect of their operation, from sales to production, from marketing to collecting payment. In order for the operation to succeed and survive, the person in control must always be present.

Before I met Megan, that was definitely me. Although often running two or three companies at a time, I had to be present and involved in absolutely all aspects of the business, which is both unsustainable and unrealistic. You can't obtain any significant level of success when you spread yourself so thin.

---

[13] "Business," *Investopedia*. July 4, 2020 (https://www.investopedia.com/terms/b/business.asp).

What follows is a brief overview of several markets you can further look into should any one of them strike a chord with you. I have personal experience in each of these industries, and my opinion is that no one business is better than the next. It's completely up to the operator and owner as to which one is of most interest and best fits your skillsets.

Internet Trading

Trading doesn't have to be limited to making timed purchases on the stock market, watching every move, and waiting for the perfect time to hit the buy or sell button. There are endless opportunities to purchase physical products and resell them on the market every day. This form of investing used to require walls in a large retail space, warehousing of goods, and face to face combat with bargain-seekers, but not anymore.

Today there are millions of people taking advantage of technology in order to purchase goods from around the world, then place them for sale on a digital marketplace, even at the hyperlocal level, such as on a community buy/sell group. While there is still some initial investment involved in acquiring goods, the investor has control over how much they spend, what they spend it on, and when they spend it.

My nephew demonstrated this type of investing when he was fifteen years old. With the assistance of his parents, he successfully located a Chinese supplier of those sensational little *spinners* that were popular a few years ago. They were permitted to purchase $100 worth of these spinners, bring them into Canada, and resell them on Kijiji.ca for a three hundred percent profit. All the while, my nephew was teaching his parents how to safely browse the web.

You certainly don't have to source your product overseas. How about those brilliant Sunday afternoon garage sales? Ever seen an item on someone's front lawn and thought, *Only $20? That thing is worth $300 all day long.* Well now, you could take the opportunity to buy it for $20 and prove yourself right.

The online landscape is changing drastically, but anyone is capable of taking advantage of this business model if it gets them excited.

Possibly the greatest benefit to buying and selling products electronically is that there's so much flexibility. If you currently enjoy a nine-to-five job but are looking to make a gradual transition into owning a business, this is a great way to do it.

Dealing in Collectibles

Perhaps you're someone who loves to make purchases but shrivels at the thought of having to sell them. A different form of investing that might fit your personality is dealing in collectibles.

Because of the amount of speculation involved in collectibles, for me this ranks right up there next to gambling in terms of risk versus reward. Too much of your success will be predicated on your ability to predict the future value of an item.

For illustration purposes, let's use the example of Coca-Cola memorabilia. Who decides the value of an iconic glass Coke bottle? What would you pay to have one sitting in your kitchen cupboard? For me, the answer is simple: "Sorry, no sale. I don't have room in my cupboards for items I don't use." The value to me is almost zero, and thus I'm not an investor in Coke bottles.

There are others, however, who would inspect the integrity of the bottle, searching the curves, cap lines, and clarity of the glass. That person might offer $50 in the hope of adding a particular bottle to their display case. Based on their perceived value, this little treasure may be worth hundreds of dollars.

Countless items are collected and resold for their intrinsic value every day. From penny candies to million-dollar cars, people collect everything.

However, one principle of business serves as a solid foundation: an item's value is determined by supply and demand. Whether you're talking about a rookie baseball card of a Hall of Famer or a signed bat that was used on the grand slam hit that won the World Series in extra innings, every item has worth—that is, if you understand supply and demand.

Arguably, this may be the most enjoyable form of investing, but returns will be heavily based on your ability to predict future demand. This can be tricky. But you could build a significant business without much money upfront.

I'm reminded of a young woman named Carmen who once purchased an inexpensive item online, a pack of sports cards, for less than $10. She began by trading the cards, not actually exchanging dollars. The initial package contained four cards, one of which happened to feature a player who'd enjoyed a notable career. In exchange for that card, Carmen was offered a Hot Wheels collectible— and she accepted the trade. She immediately reposted the Hot Wheels collectible, and within a few days she got an email from someone who would give her a remote control car that had been gently used.

Can you see where this is going? Each time Carmen agreed to make a trade, she perceived that the value of the item she was receiving was greater than the one she was giving away.

Carmen continued doing this for an entire year. Eventually, near the end of her string of trades, she had managed to take the original $10 purchase and turn it into a motorcycle. She then traded the motorcycle for a pair of Seadoos, which she subsequently traded for a boat. She then traded the boat for a fuel-efficient and safetied two-door car that proceeded to get her to school and back every day of her college career.

She was only seventeen when she completed these trades. If it hadn't been for her parents—who had told her that if she didn't want to take the bus across town to get to school, she should figure out a way to buy herself a car—then she might never have had any interest in the initial trading cards.

Small Business

This is a battlefield I've fought on since I was a young teenager. I started my first lawncare business with a used lawnmower and a weedwhacker my father had salvaged from someone else's trash. The going rate for mowing a neighbour's lawn was about $5 at the time, but I booked up my weekends, peddling around town with my equipment.

That business has survived more than thirty years and is still part of our lives today. I love business, because it can have nearly any look to it. It can happen any time of day, in nearly any part of the world, and it can be as small or as big as you'd like it to.

Fortunes have certainly been made in business even when the owner had little money to invest in it. Look at those poor college kids who tinkered with computers in their parents' garages! It's fair to say that our entire world has been changed by the impact of companies like Apple, Microsoft, and Amazon.

Regardless of who you are or where you're from, in North America you have an opportunity to start your own business. Often what starts out as a hobby or passionate pastime develops into a business model over time.

Connie worked in a fast-paced office environment and loved to come home at the end of a long day to make a hot drink after dinner. She would then knit amazingly comfortable couch blankets. It was the perfect release from her hectic nine-to-five schedule, and over the years she blessed many people with personal, custom-knitted blankets made specifically for each special person in her life.

One summer, Connie was approached by a close friend who asked if she could make a blanket for her daughter. This daughter would be leaving for university in the fall and her mother wanted to send her with something special to remember home. Soon, many other friends and family had similar requests. So Connie started taking orders.

By Christmas of that year, Connie's Covers was born. Just like that, she turned her pastime into a revenue-generating business. A single appearance at her community's seasonal craft show would fill her order book, leaving her with so much forecasted income that she decided to leave her job to pursue it full-time.

You go, girl! Take the cover off your dreams and make them all come true!

Multilevel Marketing

Perhaps you've thought of starting your own business before—and while you love the idea of being in business, you struggle with the idea of going it alone.

I was twenty years old and already had a thriving business when I was encouraged to look at another business model. The following five years would find me immersed in a business that would serve as the foundation for everything my family and I enjoy now, and it would surround me with hundreds of like-minded people all looking to make the most out of life.

Although multilevel marketing didn't result in the financial gains I hoped for in the beginning, it exposed me to personal development like no other business model had. With its emphasis on personal growth, regardless of how much money you make, you're a guaranteed winner.

My multilevel marketing business experience included a continuous diet of personal and business development books, tapes, regular meetings, seminars, and conferences. In addition, I made some pretty amazing friends along the way, people who encouraged me, supported me, and helped me learn how to develop my dreams.

How rare is that? Isn't it more common to be laughed at and ridiculed for having a dream of any proportion? Of course it is.

Have you heard the old analogy about a pail of crabs? There's no need to put a lid on a pail of crabs. Why? Because as soon as one crab reaches for the top, the others will be quick to pull it down again. So no one ever gets out.

If you feel like that sums up your life, then maybe it's time for you to find a new bucket to hang out in, and perhaps a multilevel marketing experience is what you need to help get you out of that bucket altogether.

There's another adage that says, "Products don't move people. People move products." In the mid 1960s, the DeVos family partnered with a man named

Dexter Yager, and together they created a marketing structure that would radically challenge the way products are marketed in the world.

Rather than launching huge campaigns to advertise products, they came up with the idea of network marketing. The basis of this form of marketing is that individual people market products to other people they know, who in turn market them to people they know, etc. Rather than spend billions on advertising, the sellers of the product are paid.

The reason this is called *multilevel* marketing is that the model depends on people recruiting other people who recruit still more people, creating a hierarchy of upline and downline business owners. Each person is responsible for their own business volume and are rewarded for a percentage of their own, as well as the business volume created by those whom they introduced to the business. Different companies vary in terms of commission and royalties, as well as the way in which members are educated about the market, their business, and their products.

The five years I spent in multilevel marketing was a wonderful experience. I faced more rejection in a month than most people see in their entire lives. I also spent countless hours driving from meeting to meeting and traveling long distances to attend conferences. I stayed up late, slept very little, and in the end didn't have a penny to show for my efforts.

Doesn't that sound like a wonderful business experience to you? You probably think I'm being sarcastic at this point, but truthfully, in hindsight now, with twenty years of further business experience behind me in more traditional business models, I can say with one hundred percent confidence that the experience was one of the best of my life. I made connections, had a lot of fun, and incurred minimal costs. Sure, the rejection was hard. I would share my enthusiasm with someone and they would look at me like I had three heads.

After a while, I came to realize that most people are like the crabs in that bucket I mentioned. They simply don't know any better than to pull others down. Heck, some might think they're protecting you from whatever might be on the other side of the bucket. And they do it instinctively. They don't mean to crush your dreams, it just comes naturally to them.

So the rejection hurt a lot, but guess what I learned from it? Not a single person on the planet outside of yourself can determine where you end up in life.

> Not a single person on the planet outside of yourself can determine where you end up in life.

Despite the rejection, the experience was tremendously helpful in terms of my lifelong goal to be successful in business.

Should you opt to embark on your own multilevel business journey, just be sure that you manage your expectations properly. Understand the business model and ensure that organization has business integrity.

Also, the number one motive for being in the business should be to build people up. It was repeated time and time again during my tenure in the industry, "Products don't move people. People move products. Build the people and the product sales will come." If you're not a go-it-alone kind of person, then find an organization of people like you. You may find just what you're looking for, and you may even make a little money along the way.

Purchasing an Established Business

If you feel like you lack vision, creativity, or a clear understanding of the marketplace you're interested in, all of which are strong influencers of business success, then perhaps you should consider buying a previously established business.

In our careers as investors, Megan and I have been on both sides of buying and selling businesses. Buying someone else's business has a lot of pros and cons that should be considered. But if a business already exists, then at least there's proof that there is a need for it, which eliminates some of the guesswork.

That said, any business that has been around long enough, and has served enough clients, is bound to have some baggage. Every business has it, even if you're as wholesome as a non-profit. Issues can include dissatisfied customers, outstanding liens or work orders, unpaid taxes, and disgruntled employees. So while you can forego the battle of starting an operation from scratch, you also inherit everything the prior owner may not have done properly. In business, it's often easier to defer an issue than resolve it. Left long enough, a problem that could have been relatively simple to resolve becomes difficult or complex.

When purchasing someone else's business, be sure that you understand what you're getting, the good and the bad, before the transaction closes.

Don't be discouraged when you discover the baggage, though, as treasures can often be found within that baggage. For many business owners, particularly the ones who have been operating a long time, the baggage might be so old that it's become the very reason for the sale. In reality, the business just needs some new energy, a fresh focus. You may be the very solution that business needs.

So don't be blind to the baggage, but ensure that you view it as an opportunity to add value.

This was the case with our property maintenance business. We already owned our own, but then we purchased a well-established competitor. Afterward, we quickly became one of the most significant players in the local marketplace. Overnight, we doubled the amount of equipment being deployed with our company name on it, and soon the phones were ringing off the hook. Sure, we needed to sort out some baggage, but in the end the acquisition fast-tracked our growth and positioned us as major contenders for contracts we otherwise would have been overlooked for due to our lack of resources.

If you're going to get into buying and selling businesses, it's important to trust a good lawyer—and despite popular opinion and commonly shared jokes, there are some very good lawyers out there. We've been blessed to discover one such lawyer who continually demonstrates a genuine interest in protecting us personally, as well as our businesses and what we've established.

If you need to hire a lawyer, it is recommended that you follow any advice they give you along the way. Should your lawyer suggest that a deal isn't good for you, that the documentation is heavily weighted in favour of the other side, listen to them. Stop and re-evaluate what's being proposed before you sign anything.

Almost every time our lawyer advised us to be cautious, my stubbornness led me to close the deals anyway, and he often had the opportunity to say, "I told you so." Those are painful words to hear from a guy who you pay to hear advice from. Why do you think good lawyers get paid so well? If you think it might be because they know what they're talking about, then you're right.

By the way, the same lesson applies to all areas of life: be open to the experience and wisdom of others, otherwise you'll be charged accordingly to acquire all that wisdom on your own.

Next, I want to share three specific examples of business Megan and I purchased, and you'll see that they are very different from one another. Since this book is designed to lead you to joyful finances, we want to share our experiences in hopes that they'll help you avoid your own setbacks.

First of all, you cannot maintain any focus when driving multiple businesses in completely different directions. Imagine that you're the crew chief to a NASCAR racing team. Your team's car is navigating traffic at two hundred miles per hour, solely based on your directive. Now imagine, at the same time, that you're the air traffic controller at an international airport, and jets from all around the world are landing and taking off at your command every thirty seconds. And in addition to all this, imagine that you're the dean of a world-renowned university, providing guidance to students and faculty alike.

Can you just imagine what your day would look like? With all those moving parts, how dangerous would it be to lose focus for even one second? Focus is key as you navigate your business empire, so spreading yourself too thin is a poor recipe for success.

Fortunately, Megan and I made it out alive of our stretched-too-thin business phase. Thankfully, the damage we created was manageable, and after implementing some emergency exit strategies we managed to drastically improve our focus—and as a result, improve the overall performance of all our soldiers.

Be sure to pick your battles much more carefully than we did!

Property management. Beginning in the early 2000s, I was given my first opportunity to manage a residential multifamily investment property. A year or so prior to this, the owner of the property had become a groundskeeping client of ours, and he came to recognize our reliability. On that basis alone, he thought we might be good property managers to his six residential tenants. It seemed to make sense for the owner to ask me to collect rent, fix a few things as needed, and even show vacant units from time to time. After all, I was already visiting the property weekly to cut the lawn.

I didn't foresee the business that would follow in the forthcoming years. About a decade later, my lawncare efforts had spawned a thriving property management business. We were managing tens of millions of dollars' worth of property, from single-family homes to condominium complexes. We even at one point managed a private island, which was designed to become a Canadian retreat for American owners who could afford multimillion-dollar cottages.

By the mid-2010s, we were respected as one of the top property management companies in town. However, I found that the success of our operation seemed to be a little too dependent on myself alone. I hadn't really figured out how to empower others and delegate properly, so I involved myself in every aspect of the business. I had to figure out how to let go.

Franchising. Around this time, my wife and I were strategizing about various directions we could take this arm of our business. Suddenly we learned about a property management franchise that was looking to expand across Canada. This franchise was originally from Vancouver, and after some research we learned that they were connected to some very well-known and reputable real estate companies. My research suggested that this franchise had all the answers we were looking for in terms of how to implement an established system for our team so I, as the owner, could step aside.

"It seems like a Subway sandwich shop compared to a local deli," I recall explaining to Megan. "We've already been making sandwiches for a long time, but Subway knows how to make them more consistently, and at a much greater profit."

I continued to state my case until she agreed that the opportunity was worth investigating further. At the time, we were caring for more than 250 residents. Our phones rang all the time and we'd put in place no boundaries to protect Megan or myself, not to mention our key staff. We were burning out and a franchise appeared to be the ideal solution.

Megan and I soon found ourselves on a plane headed out west with a brand-new baby in tow. During our visit to their corporate offices, we were shown eight-inch-thick binders that served as operating manuals. In order to learn all these systems, franchisees needed to graduate from an online course. We also met several members of the corporate team, ranging from IT support to sales and marketing personnel.

After returning home, all I can remember thinking is that I couldn't wait for someone to share with us how we could make our sandwiches more consistently and for more profit.

Once all the paperwork was signed, training and support staff began flying into town. Our family-owned property management business never looked the same again.

Those who operate a growing business most likely feel a flood of emotions at all times: anxiety, stress, fear, happiness, uncertainty, and excitement, just to name a few. Who *wouldn't* want to own their own business?

It is my belief that a well-established franchise system can help you reduce, but likely never eliminate, some of the painful emotions attached to business ownership. The single most wonderful benefit of a franchise is that someone else has already created the how-to manual. They've eliminated a lot of the unknowns you would normally face on a day-to-day basis if you were creating it on your own. Depending on the type of franchise, they may have their own supply chains that allow them to capitalize on economies of scale, increasing your purchasing power and simplifying the ordering process and other logistics.

For instance, in the property management business we often ran credit checks on prospective tenants, at a cost of $35 per application. The franchise we joined, however, had negotiated a national rate of just $16.95, and the information we got back was much more detailed.

Purchasing the rights to a franchise usually requires an upfront investment, a part of the decision that needs to be evaluated before entering into an agreement. Then, once the franchise rights are secured, the franchisor and franchisee develop a long-term financial relationship.

In our case, the cost to be associated with the property management franchise was equal to ten percent of our office's monthly revenue. There were fixed fees for things like software licensing, and other fees came out to simple percentages based on the type of transactions. To be certain, the franchisor will only survive if they bring in revenue, and the franchisee is their customer. This relationship is very much mutually beneficial, and it only survives if both parties remain successful.

It's important to understand all the franchising fees upfront, and how your new costs will affect your overall business model. Ask yourself how this model will impact your current customer base. Will it help you eliminate some of the trouble clients you really wish you didn't have to deal with in the first place, and replace them with the kind of clients you originally figured you would be serving when you started your business? Can your marketing budget become more effective by being combined with other franchisees' budgets in order to run regional, national, or even international campaigns?

There's a lot to consider before you jump in. However, with the proper model in place, one that has an established history of success and a support team behind it, owning a franchise can be like printing money. The mistakes have already been made, the research has been done, and the trials have been completed... all on someone else's dime.

With an understanding of the industry, you merely have to buy into someone else's proven model of success and emulate what they've done. You, too, can then become a successful business owner—in time.

In terms of our larger metaphor in this book, this would be an example of a battlefield whereby you send your troops into battle under the seasoned leadership of a general who already understands the landscape and has won here before. Success is never guaranteed, but with good leadership and experienced training, your troops will stand a much greater chance at winning.

A final consideration when purchasing a franchise is to ensure that your lawyer reviews the terms and conditions of the franchise agreement. Be certain that you understand the commitment you're making and all the associated revenues and costs. If you're unsure, ask your lawyer or the franchisor for greater clarification. Only once you have a comfortable understanding should you move forward with the agreement. After you commit is bad time to encounter surprises and misunderstandings.

Inflatable rentals. With all that was going on in our business portfolio, Megan and I faced the constant struggle of acquiring and maintaining good staff.

Throughout our tenure as business owners, we hired more than one hundred people ranging from high school students to second-career retirees. We got to meet a lot of very interesting people. Sadly, when our employees inevitably left, we'd have to fill the hole.

Our desire to avoid this situation is one reason why we decided to venture into the business of inflatable rentals.

At the time this opportunity found me, I shouldn't have been looking for another business to run. We had a lot on our plate, most of which was growing and doing well—but as they say, "Once an entrepreneur, always an entrepreneur."

One evening, I was browsing the internet for businesses that were for sale and came across an inflatable rental business. At first glance, I wasn't the least bit interested. But as I read further, it appeared to be something rather unique.

After reading the ad a third time, I nudged Megan, who was sitting next to me after a long day at the office. "Honey, I think I found another business we should look at…"

I'm sure you can picture her enthusiasm. She was exhausted at the time. I myself had nothing left in the tank most days, since we already had four or five companies on the go. We also had two children, both under the age of two… so what was I doing suggesting that we start yet another business?

"You're kidding, right?" Megan retorted sluggishly.

"I know it sounds crazy, but hear me out. They're selling a business model that would actually make our lives simpler."

Looking back now, I think that was consistently my belief. It always seemed to me that the next business would be the one that really made things work for us. I had been feeling like something was missing. I couldn't put my finger on it, but it caused me to keep looking in the hope that one day I would stumble upon the solution.

The most interesting aspect of this inflatable rental business was that they weren't offering a brick-and-mortar business. The seller was suggesting that if you purchased this massive inflatable arena they had, the largest inflatable device of its kind, then they would handle all the marketing and booking in exchange for a twenty percent share of each rental agreement price. They would canvas the area for clients, run ads, field phone calls, and negotiate dates and hours—and in exchange, our responsibility would include delivery, setup, babysitting the equipment while onsite, and removing it at the end of the rental period.

As a business owner all too familiar with the cost of hiring staff, source deductions, and benefits, etc., I immediately recognized that we would never be able to hire someone in a support role for the amount we'd be paying them to generate leads and make bookings. It seemed like a really good deal.

Just a few weeks later, we took delivery of our massive inflatable arena. This gigantic display stood sixteen feet tall and was twenty feet wide by forty feet long. When we set it up in the parking lot of our power equipment store, it turned heads and got the attention we were looking for.

Well, everything doesn't always go according to plan… but hey, that's the life of an entrepreneur. We constantly make the best of things.

Although we had done our due diligence prior to purchasing this business, we learned shortly after our product arrived that the business support model being offered was a scam. When we inquired about when the bookings would begin, because obviously we had very busy schedules and this was something new we would have to work around, we were immediately advised that the company no longer serviced our area.

That's right. These people sold us the overpriced bouncing platform, got their money, and then moved on to the next area. They got away with ten times the cost of the equipment.

Before you decide to buy into a support partnership, it's crucial that you find out what other support they're already providing and confirm its effectiveness. If you aren't fully satisfied with the information you get, trust your instinct and walk away from the deal.

In the process of investigating this opportunity, there had been several red flags. However, we'd viewed them as yield signs only, and so we had slowed down but kept moving forward. But as I wrote earlier, if your lawyer starts waving a red flag at you, take your yellow-tinted sunglasses off and listen to their advice.

Public service. When we were preparing to give birth to our third child, a very unique business opportunity was presented to us. There was an office in our town that provided government-related services, and it had been contracted out to a private operator who was ready to retire. I clearly remember Megan telling me that this might be a bad idea. This was her third pregnancy inside twenty-one months, and we had enough on our plate. But I thought I'd gotten pretty good at handling things, so I didn't see the reason for her concern.

I must have been crazy. We had two children in diapers, were expecting a third, and already had businesses stacked on top of businesses. But true to my character, I disregarded any sign of wisdom, neglected to heed our lawyer's warnings, and once again moved forward.

This business operated according to a model quite different from most in that its income came from the government, not customers. However, at the end of the day the operations very much resembled that of a traditional franchise model. Strict policies and procedures were already in place and, like a franchise, we would simply need to implement the already established practices.

In order to run the branch, we were provided with our inventory. All the other requirements were our responsibility as the business owners. Our preparations included renting an office space, filling it with the appropriate furniture, and employing staff. After a long process of government officials training our team, we were provided with detailed manuals on the business's policies and procedures and how to complete each type of transaction.

Because the office systems were connected directly to government agencies, our income was automated. We received a commission from every transaction we performed.

We initially thought this was wonderful. However, because Megan and I already had some experience in the business world, we quickly noticed a few very difficult aspects of this model. Training new employees was extensive and therefore very costly. We also realized that it was difficult to retain trustworthy employees, as the commission payments we received weren't great enough for us to offer competitive wages or benefit packages.

Another challenge with working in partnership with the government was that when we saw the need or opportunity for improvements, they were impossible to implement. All the operations, right down to the hours we were allowed to be open, were part of a large government infrastructure that included layers of bureaucracy.

Additionally, although the daily transactions were reported automatically, we also discovered that the amount of monitoring required by the government forced us to constantly dedicate time to non-revenue-generating reporting and submissions.

We quickly determined that the government-backed business model had some very costly flaws. Over time, it proved to be financially unstable for us.

So there you have it—three completely different business models, in different industries entirely, all being owned and operated simultaneously by the same owners. The lessons we learned during this time were frequent, expensive, and both physically and mentally crushing.

It took two years of managing this situation and the three babies before we collapsed. And make no mistake about it, we *collapsed*. All the warnings our lawyer had given us ultimately proved accurate. My wife had known better than to get involved in all these opportunities, but I had been so focused on my perceived success that I hadn't listened.

There are a lot of benefits to starting a new business, and among them is the fact that they offer incredible tax advantages, freedom in terms of one's time, and potential streams of income that can lead to a myriad of opportunities. The key to all this is not to go it alone but to have trusted, selfless advisors. These are hard to find, but I do believe they exist. When you find a professional you can trust, quickly determine how to add them to your army, then respect their time and honour their knowledge every chance you can.

You may be thinking that both paper investing and business have done my family wrong based on the stories I've shared thus far. Truthfully, though, these tools have all been incredibly rewarding.

But most of our recent success, happiness, and freedom has come in large part due to real estate. Join me in the next chapter as we investigate this industry in greater detail and see how real estate provided me and my wife a jobless lifestyle before I turned forty and she turned thirty-four.

Freshen your coffee. This next chapter might be my favourite yet!

10

The Real Estate Battlefield

Hear another parable. There was a master of a house who
planted a vineyard and put a fence around it and dug a winepress
in it and built a tower and leased it to tenants,
and went into another country.
(Matthew 21:33, ESV)

There are millions of people who make millions of dollars every year using the very tools I have outlined in the last two chapters. But there are equally as many who are rebounding, recovering, or still on the emotional sidelines because they jumped into the "deal of a lifetime" only to have it go south—and by south, I'm not talking about tropical islands. The same can be said about real estate as an investment.

However, because of the unmatched joy and freedom we have personally experienced through real estate, we are about to unpack how we started with a two-bedroom, one-bathroom rental house and turned it into a life of financial freedom before the age of forty.

Welcome to what I consider to be my most enjoyable chapter in the book. In the following pages, we'll provide you some insight as to how we were able to completely change our lifestyles, enjoy our children more, and strengthen our already solid marriage. Through years of passionately and persistently pursuing education on this battlefield, we've positioned ourselves to win an increasingly large percentage of our battles here.

Real estate has proven to be a tool capable of buying back our time, reducing our stress, enhancing our perspective on life, and overall allowing us to optimize our joy in wealth, finance, wellness, faith, family and friends, and in every other aspect of our lives. We are so grateful for what investing in real estate has allowed us to do.

The year was 1998. I had just completed a machine shop program at the local college and accepted a job at a manufacturing plant for a staggering $7.25 per hour. I was running my lawncare business, which was heading into its sixth season, and by this point I had added two helpers who would cut grass at my clients' properties during the day while I put in hours at the machine shop.

Once the whistle blew and I could break away from my job, I joined up with the guys and cut grass until dark. We were making more than $15 per hour, so it seemed like great money in comparison to my day job.

But the ambition of a focused twenty-two-year-old should never be underestimated. As if working from 7:00 a.m. to nearly 10:30 p.m., often six days a week, wasn't enough, I was also exposed to multilevel marketing during this time. It opened my mind to a completely different kind of income generation. As they say, "Your mind is like an elastic. Once it is stretched, it never returns to its original state."

Although I didn't mind working eighty hours a week, I was still living at my parents' home and had little to no responsibilities in life as far as managing a home of my own, a family, etc. I could see that working so many hours wasn't sustainable for the long-term.

In my early twenties, like most people that age, I figured I was unstoppable. At twenty-five, I trained and successfully completed the *Detroit Free Press* marathon, because my sister had joked at Christmas the year prior that my butt was getting a little chunky. Challenge accepted!

Eighteen weeks of training for the 26.2-mile run solidified in my mind everything that I had been reading and listening to during those first two years of multilevel marketing training, and the three more that would follow. Because of my access to their support network, I was able to purchase motivational and educational books, tapes, and even seminar tickets on a weekly, monthly, and quarterly basis. I was a passionate consumer of personal self-help materials, business development strategies, financial planning books, and even relationship building tools. Was I perfect? Of course not—not then, nor now—but I was still a kid in the world.

The biggest challenge I had to overcome, which is the same challenge many have to overcome in life, was my own attitude. I had developed belief systems in my first twenty-five years that were flat-out lies. Perhaps some of these apply to you today:

- The person who does the best job is the one who will come out on top.
- How others perceive me is who I am.
- Title and status determine my worth.
- The more my job pays me, the more important I will be and the more people will like me.
- If you're nice most of the time, you'll go to heaven.
- Life is fair.
- If you work hard until you're sixty-five, someone will take care of you financially until the day you die.

If any of these statements ring true for you today, that's okay. Realize, however, that in order to succeed at any level in life, it's critical that those lies be abolished.

The only way I was able to do that was by reading, listening, and surrounding myself with people who were of a similar mindset. You certainly won't become a successful and joyful person by watching television or picking up those magazines conveniently located at the end of grocery store checkout lines. Those aren't the type of materials I'm referring to.[14]

In my fourth year of multilevel marketing, I was blessed to hear Robert Kiyosaki speak at a major conference. Sitting in an auditorium of more than twenty-five thousand people, it seemed as though he was speaking directly to me that night, as if there was no one else in the room. I hung on every word as he quickly explained that through his investments in real estate he had successfully replaced all his earned income and was able to work from home, travel regularly, teach others, and spend more time with his wife Kim. At that time, Kiyosaki would have only been about forty-five years old.

I couldn't believe my ears. Here I was, working like a madman, doing some pretty backbreaking labour. While I was making pretty good money, I always knew that the income was directly related to my unsustainable efforts and that

---

[14] Books like the one in your hand now are designed to encourage, inspire, and educate. This is a great start. No single book will have all the answers you're looking for, so when you're through with this book, perhaps after reading it four or five times, I encourage you to find another title that attracts you and read it as well.

as soon as I decided to take my foot off the gas pedal, my income would drop drastically.

By the time Kiyosaki's seminar presentation found me, I had read more than a hundred books on all areas of self-help and business development. I was ready to hear what he was saying. When I heard the term *passive income*, I knew I had to learn more.

Immediately following his presentation, I went to the concourse to find his booth and stand in line to purchase his first book. *Rich Dad, Poor Dad* came home with me that weekend. In the years that followed, it found its place on my bookshelves along with dozens of books Kiyosaki would either author, co-author, or recommend. I affectionately named this collection my "purple library," after the colour scheme of all his books.

It's fair to say that I haven't adopted every word Kiyosaki shared as gospel, nor would I suggest that you do that with any of the material you read. What Kiyosaki's materials did extremely well, however, was open my mind to the possibilities of becoming wealthy, working fewer hours, living where I wanted to (instead of where it was convenient), and spending more time with my family. These were all goals I had been carrying with me since high school. Until Kiyosaki introduced me to real estate, I hadn't had any idea how I was going to get there.

Let's take a look at some of the realities about real estate investing that have made a difference in my life.

Top Ten Things I Like About Real Estate

1. The market changes very slowly. I think this is an advantage to most investors. Generally speaking, the value of real estate does fluctuate, but changes in value take months—not minutes. If you're a busy person and don't have time to watch the stock value of Company XYZ, that's okay. Property that's purchased for $100,000 today is likely still going to be worth the same thing when you wake up the next morning. Sleep well. You haven't missed your big chance to cash out your profit.

2. You control the value. Possibly the greatest benefit for an investor like myself is that owners can directly affect the value of their property by deciding to make improvements or defer maintenance. Should you purchase a property for $100,000 and wish to increase its value, you may choose to update the curb appeal with some fresh new landscaping. Sometimes this just means pulling weeds and mowing the lawn. Or perhaps you want to go through with a pail of paint and freshen up the interior. A little sweat equity and suddenly you could see an increased value in your investment by thousands of dollars.

For the more ambitious investor, renovating bathrooms and kitchens can be a little more expensive and time-consuming, but the value of a property is significantly affected by the condition of these two rooms.

On commercial properties where the tenant is generally responsible for all the interior maintenance, an investor can increase the value by improving the parking area, installing a patio, or changing out the facade to make the building more attractive.

3. Property value appreciation. In the event you purchase and hold onto a piece of property but decide you're not the fixer-upper type, the value will still increase as long as you regularly maintain the property—including groundskeeping and general repair. Why can we predict that with any confidence? The reason is that land is a limited resource, and yet the population of the world continues to grow each year. Regardless of where you are in the world, or where you'd like to invest in real estate, there's a strong chance that property values will be greater in ten years than they are today, simply because of supply and demand.

4. Tax implications. If you're a hard-working person who earns a high income, you undoubtedly have some strong feelings about how much money you pay the government in income tax. It's important to pay the taxes you owe, but through education you'll come to learn that there are very important laws in place which permit high-income earners, investors, and corporations to reduce the amount of income tax they're subject to paying each year. It's very much worth learning about the tax benefits of owning investment real estate.

One important disclaimer needs to be made at this point. Tax laws vary in every region, and are constantly changing. I make no claim to being an accountant, so it's critically important that you form a team of qualified professionals that can work with you to maximize the benefits of your investments.

This cannot be overstated. I've met people who tell me with pride that they've saved money each year because they did their own taxes online and didn't have to pay an accountant to assist. But good accountants do a lot more than just process your income tax return, and from personal experience I can assure you that they will be well worth hiring if they're able to set you on a proper path of increased income and reduced taxes. Expenses related to your investment real estate, such as professional fees, property tax, building maintenance or improvements, repairs, advertising, and tenant appreciation gifts can often be deducted from your personal income taxes and provide a nice backend benefit for you as an investor. You have to know the laws, or other people who know them, in order to put them to work for your advantage.

5. Cashflow. This concept is the king of all kings in the investment world. When one invests in paper assets, a common goal is to create a future cashflow that will offset or compensate a person for their reduced income in retirement. In the event that someone invests $5,000 per year for twenty years prior to retirement—for instance, in a vehicle such as an RRSP or 401K—they won't take any money from the investment until later in life, although their money manager might have to in order to cover fees.

The goal from the start is to create enough of a base investment that when the investor retires and no longer has their monthly income, they can subsidize it with a small draw from the funds they've squirreled away for the past twenty years. Perhaps the value of that investment has blossomed to a generous $160,000 by the time they're ready to begin withdrawing their cashflow. Sadly, each month that they pull funds from the account, the account balance is likely to decline in direct proportion to the withdrawal—and thus, the ongoing earning power of that investment is reduced.

By contrast, one of the greatest benefits to investing in real estate is that although the investor may begin with a $100,000 property, in which they invest as little as $5,000, the rent payments will provide positive cashflow, as long as it's greater than the expenses incurred to manage and maintain the property. Rather than the cashflow reducing the investment's value or earning power, investors will often assess the value of the real property based on how much cashflow it produces.

For example, if you happen to purchase a vacant single-family home for $100,000 as an investment property and then give it some improved curb appeal and a coat of paint, you may be able to rent it out for $200 a month net profit. In a situation like this, not only would you find that you suddenly had an additional income stream, you would quickly learn that the value of your investment had gone up, not down.

If the real estate market didn't change one penny in the same twenty-year period, the real estate investor would have enjoyed a $48,000 cashflow benefit without the value of the property going down. In this scenario, the investor would be able to increase their rate by about one percent per year, while the property value could increase by two percent. The operating costs, such as mortgage payments, tend to go down over time, as do factors such as turnover and maintenance, as you gain skills related to property ownership and management.

Peter did exactly this. He purchased a small single-family home for $100,000 by putting five percent down, or $5,000, and mortgaging the balance owing. He rented the home out and after his expenses were paid out each month he had a balance of $200 left over for himself. This $200 is called his monthly cashflow.

Early on, he and I had several conversations about whether it was worth the hassle for just $200 per month. Twenty years later, however, when Peter decided to cash out, his monthly cashflow had increased to more than $525 per month, due to reduced expenses and increased rental rates. Plus, the sale price of the property was more than $285,000.

You certainly don't have to be an accountant to understand that getting a return like that on a $5,000 investment, even without taking into account the tax benefits he realized during the twenty years he held the investment, is an amazing deal.

6. The shopping process. It's not common that you would find yourself at a social event and overhear someone captivating the room with a story about how they spent the previous week sitting at their computer looking at spreadsheets and performance charts. To my knowledge, my wife is the only person I know who begins to shake with excitement at the word *spreadsheet*.

This explains why most people who invest in paper assets such as stocks and bonds tend to hand their money over to someone who gets paid to sit and look through all that information for them. It's boring. No one would do it for free.

Let's talk real estate shopping, though. This is when I sit up straight and turn my ear.

"Did you say real estate shopping?" you may ask.

Yeah, baby. Where are we going? How about Hawaii? What about Vancouver? Have you ever seen Costa Rica? There are real estate opportunities everywhere you go, and once you decide to pursue them, you can begin going to all these places to look at potential investments. In fact, you can consider the cost of doing so to be tax-deductible.

Doesn't that seem a little more exciting than sitting at your desk?

I can hear you saying, "Sure, that's great. But I'm not buying property in Hawaii any time soon."

Maybe not, but shopping is so much fun, even when the purpose is just to learn what other markets have to offer compared to the one you're investing in.

Let's get more local, because it's wise to start small and close to home. Wouldn't it be fun to spend a day seeing all the properties in your hometown?

What unique features can you find? Why are people in your area selling right now? How does your home compare to the ones you might invest in as a rental?

You'll also find that as you spend more time looking at real estate, whether you're ready to spend or just window-shopping, your vision of what is possible will grow. When I first brought Megan on board to my real estate adventures, she turned in disgust at some of the addresses we looked at. Now, however, after years of experience, we laugh as we walk through properties, which some would consider to be knockdowns, and say aloud the same things about the potential we see.

Education really is the greatest investment an investor can make. While you're shopping for real estate, whether you purchase a property right then or not, any costs related to shopping are tax-deductible and the knowledge you gain could serve you for years to come. Ain't that better than staring at spreadsheets?

7. Leverage, doing more with less. Leverage should be considered the eighth wonder of the world. In investor terms, it ties the phrase *compounding interest* in importance. And when you can marry the two... look out!

So what is leverage? Unlike most paper assets, real estate has a universally understood value to financial institutions and private money holders alike. Because of this, investors are often able to partner with a lender to acquire more investment than their personal bank account would qualify them for.

As an example, many first-time homebuyers would qualify for a five percent down mortgage which essentially permits them to own a $100,000 property for as little as $5,000. The amazing thing about this is that although the lender charges a fixed cost—for example, a four percent interest rate on the loan—if the property cashflows or increases in value, the investor keeps one hundred percent of that benefit.

Imagine that you purchased that $100,000 property and a year later you had collected net rents of $200 per month in positive cashflow. Additionally, imagine that you now learn that the value of real estate in the area has appreciated two percent since you bought it. While the lender would get his four percent return, which you've paid for with the rent and calculated into your net cashflow, you would have earned $2,400 in cashflow as well as an additional $2,000 in capital equity increase.

Before you even consider factoring the tax benefits related to the cost of the four percent interest you paid the lender, you've already earned $4,400 on your $5,000 cash investment. That's an eighty-eight percent return! The lender got *four* percent.

Can you see why leverage is so incredible? Imagine what your financial future would look like if you enjoyed one hundred percent returns year after year for the next twenty years.

8. Government incentives. One of the things that marks real estate as such an obvious investment opportunity is that the government is willing to provide incentives to the investor.

When an investor purchases two hundred shares of stock in Company XYZ, what is their purpose? To generate a profit from a future sale, generally. That's about the only intent.

While profit may be a significant motive for a real estate investor, the investor is also likely to fill two needs for the community. One, they'll improve the condition of the property, thus making the surrounding community more attractive. Two, they use the property to provide a person, family, or business a place to live.

Providing housing is viewed as an important community service in the eyes of the government, which is why government grants, low-interest loans, and a host of tax deductions are available to the investor who opts to use their property investment in this manner.

Let me share an example from a small town of approximately twenty-five thousand people. Our investment group discovered a mixed-use commercial building that was very rundown and tired. However, it was sitting directly inside the town's Community Improvement Plan (CIP) zone. After acquiring the property, we had the building inspected, spoke to the municipality about what kinds of improvements would qualify for their CIP funding, and inside of one year we had completed nearly $100,000 worth of improvements based on their recommendation.

Following completion, the municipal inspector visited the property to confirm the quality of the improvements. Once he reported back to the CIP administrators, our improvement costs were paid back to us at a rate of nearly fifty percent.

The post improvement appraisal showed that the building had increased in value by nearly $225,000 in a little over eighteen months. How's that for doing more with less? And the government provided half of the cost to make a difference in the community. What was once referred to as the ugly building on the street became a place that tenants proudly called home. It really was a win/win situation.

So you can invest in something that improves the community, has the backing of the government, and can generate wealth.

9. Teamwork. When I met my wife, she was working as a chartered accountant at a very popular and busy firm. I had three businesses on the go at the time, although they were small enough that I could manage them while only being local two weeks of each month. The other two weeks I had to travel about twelve and a half hours away by car.

The year before I met Megan, I capitalized on an opportunity to purchase some very inexpensive houses that needed a lot of work, but they were half a day away, in another country. Being single, without any kids, and having some freedoms afforded to me by my business, I made it my mission to spend two weeks at home tending to life—my business, my home, paying bills etc.—and then I would hit the road for two weeks.

Shortly after we met, I invited her down to see what I was doing. This was a hysterical trip that warrants further sharing at some point, but anyhow, she stayed for the first week and then had to get back to the office. After all, tax returns simply don't file themselves.

When I returned following the second week, I could tell Megan had been thinking about our trip quite a bit. After just a few days of catchup, I mentioned to her again that I was preparing for my next trip—and when I suggested she could come again anytime she wanted, the wheels in her mind began to race.

But as I watched her facial expressions shift, she went from appearing confused to disappointed.

"What's the matter?" I asked.

"I can't get that much time off. Which sucks, because it was way more fun than sitting in my cubicle every day."

Not long after returning from my next trip, Megan the planner had an idea. We married that spring, and soon after she resigned from her position at the firm, becoming our bookkeeper and my most trusted handywoman partner. We decided that together we would be a much more effective real estate team, and since that time we've purchased dozens of units, completed countless projects and improvements, and yes, visited those properties without having to burn vacation pay.

Working as a husband and wife team has drastically improved the joy we extract from our real estate investing business, and it's certainly the thing I enjoy most about real estate investing. Whether we win or lose, we both get our hands dirty, crunch numbers, and go through the emotions together.

Real estate really does have something for everyone, so partners coming into this industry aren't required to be specialists in order to get started. The gifts and talents you have right now are more than enough to start. Make a commitment to constant improvement and growth, and in no time at all you'll have a show-stopping team capable of building the future you want!

> The gifts and talents you have right now are more than enough to start.

10. Generational business. For the investor who has a much bigger picture in mind than just making some profit in their own lifetime, one of the biggest benefits of investing in real estate is the ability to develop it over multiple generations. It's an incredible feeling to know that my children, and possibly even their children, will benefit from what I'm building today.

Imagine your children watching you work sixty to eighty hours per week for the better part of forty years only to one day hear you say, "Okay, I'm done with it now. It's all yours." Can you picture the somersaults and cartwheels they would be doing to understand you've just sentenced them to the same misery you endured your whole life?

This certainly doesn't have to be the case for committed real estate investors.

Although the market does change slowly, over time it's possible to amass large values of real estate, millions of dollars' worth, if you really want to go after it for a while. So what would it look like if by the time you were fifty years old, you and your spouse decided that you simply had more than you needed? Five, ten, maybe even twenty million dollars in real estate investments could produce tens of thousands of dollars in rent each month.

Now imagine that same conversation with your children.

"Well, your mother and I have been discussing it. Frankly, we just don't need all that we've acquired in our real estate portfolio. So we've decided to give you two million dollars' worth of property to get you started. The monthly cashflow from those properties is about $8,000 after expenses. It will require you to spend a couple hours each month taking care of administration, but as you know, we've been managing those tasks from various places around the world—so you won't be tied down to a desk somewhere."

The excitement comes from realizing that if you're lucky enough to live that long, you may just see your children take what you've built from nothing and turn it into multiple times the investment portfolio you provided them as a quick start. And what do you think they'll be able to do with their portfolio when they decide they're done with it? You guessed it—they'll get the third generation involved to see how much more they can do with what the first two generations built.

Wow! What a wonderful thought that would be to consider next time you look at your child or grandchild. You may be the very reason they become ultra-rich one day.

Build, Protect, Grow, Deploy, Give Away

Throughout this book, we've made reference to your money being like soldiers in an army, which we have to care for and protect, and lead into battle strategically.

But what weapons are you providing your soldiers? I consider paper assets, such as stocks or bonds, to be like swords and handguns, but real estate is like owning a combat tank and a bomber jet plane. It's the heavy artillery. And clearly, the more effectively your army is armed, the greater their chances of success on the battlefield.

Wouldn't it be wonderful if you could equip an entire army, train them how to perform with or without your continued leadership, and then hand them down to your family so they can benefit from it?

In the last few pages I've listed the top ten reasons that I prefer to invest my time, money, and personal energy in real estate. Do all the other investments have a place? Of course they do, but when you stack up the pros and cons of all the different options out there, it's my strong opinion that anyone willing to take the time to educate themselves in investing, as opposed to simply handing over their money, will see better long-term results in real estate than any other marketplace. And if they're fortunate enough, they may even have the opportunity to leave a legacy that will continue for generations not yet born.

"But I don't have any money!" you may say.

Contrary to popular belief among the working class, money is available to those who seek it. The first step in getting some is to get educated. Congratulations. You're on the right track. Stick with us as we'll discuss various means of financing in the following chapter.

PART
A Deeper Look
THREE

11

Ins and Outs

The fear of the Lord is the beginning of knowledge,
but fools despise wisdom and instruction.
(Proverbs 1:7, NKJV)

Up to this point, we've discussed the basics of running your home or small business. We've introduced a way to view money in terms of an army prepared to go to battle. We've also discussed various forms of investments.

As we work through this third section of the book, we're going to look at some finer distinctions within the financial arena. These areas are often overlooked and frequently misunderstood, yet they can each have a tremendous impact on your financial joy in life.

In this section, you'll learn about the difference between an asset and a liability, as well as the difference between good debt and bad debt. You'll be introduced to various lending sources, with explanations and examples of when you might approach them. Finally, we'll conclude with two powerful chapters that discuss the debt reduction strategies that have helped us out over the years. You'll also learn how to convert bad debt into good debt while simultaneously building an investment portfolio right now—not in two, three, five, or ten years.

Get yourself comfortable and let's get to it. There's still a lot to cover.

Assets and Liabilities[15]

I give Robert Kiyosaki all the credit for teaching me the distinction between assets and liabilities. Back in Chapter Two, we looked at certain words that trigger emotions in us and affect how we process information.

Well, until I learned the truth about assets and liabilities, the only emotion I felt when hearing these two words was confusion.

To eliminate confusion, Kiyosaki uses a litmus test to every item that quickly determines whether it's an asset or a liability. It works one hundred percent of the time, no exceptions. Simply ask this one question: does this put money in my pocket or take money out of my pocket?

Simple, right? That's it.

You may be thinking at this point, *Don't tell me the house I live in isn't an asset. It's gone up forty-two percent in value since we moved in.*

So does your house put money in your pocket or take it out of your pocket? Your house takes money out of your pocket, doesn't it? Even in the event that you owned it free and clear, you're still obligated to pay property tax, electricity, gas, maintenance, and even throw in the occasional new appliance. This all takes money out of your pocket, and thus, even if your house is mortgage-free, it's a liability to you while you live in it.

Those last words—*while you live in it*—are the key here. During that time, your house is still an asset, true, but to whom?

If you have a mortgage, your home is an asset of the bank, because they make interest on your loan. The municipality also counts your home among its assets, because they collect tax dollars from you each year. It's also an asset to the utility companies, as they profit on your need to consume their services.

You get the picture, right? While you live in it, your home is *an* asset, just not *your* asset.

Now, what happens when you sell or rent out your home? Suddenly that house becomes your asset as well—either because you sell it for more than you owe and post a net gain, or because it rents for more money each month than your financial obligations to own it. Either way, you begin to benefit from it financially.

If this doesn't sit well with you, please allow some time to absorb this new idea. It's a radical mindset shift to go from thinking of your house as an investment to realizing it's actually a liability for most of the time that you own it.

---

[15] Because understanding this distinction is such a basic foundation to experiencing financial joy, we've covered these concepts quite thoroughly in my prior book. Here we're just going to recap that explanation. I encourage you to read *Joyful Wealth* if additional clarity is still required.

Let me add one final thought to ensure you don't get the wrong message here. Like many liabilities, your home is necessary and can be a tremendous investment, so please don't think that it's all bad for you and that you should refrain from owning one. The important thing here is that you grasp the distinction between asset and liability as it applies to everything you purchase.

Although the home you live in, unless a portion is rented out, is a liability, what are some other assets you may own now or purchase in the future? There are stocks, bonds, and mutual funds, although because of their volatility they can be liabilities as well. Rental property, businesses, and franchises are all assets. Of course, how well they perform is dependent on how well they're managed. Should you opt to build a business on your own, it may be a liability until you obtain enough education to operate it profitably, after which it'll put money in your pocket each month and thus become an asset for you.

What other common errors do people tend to make? Many believe their car is an asset, or their sports memorabilia collection, or even the pool they've installed in their backyard. After all, a contractor may confirm that having one behind an Arizona home will increase the value of the property by more than what the pool costs.

But based on the definitions we've looked at, how would you classify that pool? It's a liability, right? Of course. And here are a couple of reasons why. First, the contractor isn't going to install it for free, so that's one way money will leave your pocket. Second, pools need maintenance—chlorine, salt, filter sand, the list goes on. That's money out of your pocket the entire time you own it. Lastly, although the contractor may not have lied when he said the pool would increase your property value, did he take into account that you were planning to live there for another ten to twenty years before putting it on the market? By the time you decide to sell, the pool may be very well used. Will you still get more value than it cost to install? In a lot of circumstances, no.

In fact, as a professional real estate investor myself, we often evaluate homes with a pool as being less valuable than those without. Of course there are some exceptions, but if you install a pool with the belief that you're investing in an asset, you may want to re-evaluate the purchase before putting a shovel in the ground.

Before we move forward, I'd like to encourage you to complete a quick exercise.

On a blank sheet of paper, go ahead and write down all the high-value items that you keep in your possession. Write down anything with a perceived dollar value of more than $1,000. Beside the item, write down whether you think it's an asset or liability. Finally, call to mind how you paid for each item. Did you borrow? Did you save after-tax dollars until you could afford it? Did you spend pre-taxed dollars?

When you're done, look at the paper with a new appreciation for the difference between assets and liabilities. What do you notice? If you're like me, and most of the people I speak to about this topic, you may realize that the majority of the high-value items in your life are liabilities. Cars, motorcycles, your home, a cottage, the latest technology… none of these things are assets. And most of the time, people are quick to borrow money to acquire them, either by going to the bank and asking for a loan or simply pulling out the plastic and charging it.

I personally think the modern-day credit card epidemic occurred because it removed personal accountability. How easy is it to pull out a card at the checkout counter and walk away with your purchases? It's easier than going to the bank and explaining that you need a $1,000 loan to buy a new vibrating chair. Wouldn't you expect the banker to look at you with a half-cocked head and say, "Have you considered getting off the chair and finding a job?"

Not anymore. No more must we be judged by bankers trying to protect us. We just pull out our credit card and charge it. Every credit card issuer out there wants you to believe you're worth that big purchase—*now!*

And then came internet shopping. Now you don't even have to justify your purchase to the cashier anymore. You get that liability delivered directly to your door without a second thought. That is, until the credit card statement arrives.

> …most people spend their entire working careers buying up liabilities under the false belief that they're actually investing in assets…

Would you believe that most people spend their entire working careers buying up liabilities under the false belief that they're actually investing in assets? When their working days are over, they realize too late that the only way to capitalize on what they've been buying all their lives is to sell it. You sell your house and get the equity. You sell your car, your boat, and whatever else you thought you would enjoy in your golden years… But wait, aren't you going to need a place to live, a vehicle to get around in, and something to do with the newfound freedom of your retirement? Of course you will, but all you'll be left with after the sale is a bunch of cash. Does that seem like a good plan? Not at all.

Equipped with your new understanding of assets and liabilities, I encourage you to invest your hard-earned after-tax dollars, *borrowing money when needed*, to acquire assets. Then allow your assets to pay for your liabilities. This may very well be the formula that sets your life on a new path to joyful finances.

Good Debt

When is it okay to get a loan? There are times when you would be encouraged to take on debt to improve your financial joy. Yes, you read that sentence correctly.

It may appear like a contradiction at first, particularly if you came from a culture that suggests that all debt is bad and your primary financial goal in life is to be debt-free. For investors like myself, the goal of being debt-free is secondary. Sure, it would be wonderful not to owe anyone anything, but at what cost would you want to find yourself in that position?

There is a commonly shared principle of duplication that can be illustrated using a penny that doubles in value every day for a month. The question is proposed: which would you rather have, $1,000,000 right now, or a penny that doubles in value every day for a month? While the $1,000,000 instant offer is very attractive, the value of the penny, when doubled each day for an entire month, equates to tens of millions of dollars by the end.

Now imagine being able to apply the principle of the doubling penny to a lot more money, even if the money wasn't entirely yours. Remember that the cost of borrowing is generally fixed, but the investor is the one who reaps the lion's share of the growth and gains.

Let's have a look at the cost of becoming debt-free and determine whether that's a price you really want to pay.

As you leave the security of your parents' home, you generally begin to establish your own financial army—although you start off with very few soldiers. You may enter the battle armed with an education, ready and eager to trade time, a resource you perceive to be abundantly available, for the opportunity to gather more soldiers, in the form of a paycheque.

For your first few years of independence, week in and week out, the romance of this new world is filled with excitement and learning, like with any new relationship. It's incredibly difficult to establish your own home base, so it's a very slow build. Too many people claim, "I'll get started as soon as my school debt is paid, my car is paid for, and I have a house that I want. Then I'll start saving." That day becomes ever elusive as the years go by. The new job becomes old. The school debt gets replaced by a second car payment. The house you buy comes with a mortgage equal to the maximum amount the bank would lend you. Soon you have some new expenses to deal with—such as diapers, field trips, and family vacations. Just like that, you have a host of reasons to wait before building your army.

Sound familiar? If not for your own family, then it's true for both your neighbours and more than one half of your family. According to Erica Alini of Global News Canada, recent studies show that more than fifty percent of Canadians are $200 or less away from not being able to pay their monthly bills.[16] Where is the joy in that? And how do we stop the madness?

Build an army early, or borrow one, that will fight for you.

Children remain living at their parents' home base later in life these days. The majority don't leave Mom and Dad's nest until they're in their mid-twenties, if not later, so they certainly have the opportunity to build an army before they branch out—if they're taught to implement the needed financial discipline at a young age.

For those who have already spread their wings and left the nest, in most cases the amount of money they make individually isn't enough to simultaneously build their own home base and an army of soldiers. So why not borrow the army? That's right. Let someone else's army fight the good fight for you and take the victories from those borrowed battle seekers and build your own platoon.

Now, I'm not suggesting that you borrow an army so you can buy yourself a second home in the tropics somewhere. Let your own army do that. My suggestion is to borrow an army so you can put them to work acquiring assets for you now rather than later. This is exactly what the term leverage means, which we discussed earlier. A borrowed fleet of fighters allows you to collect, build, and grow much faster than you could on our own individual effort.

In case you haven't connected all the dots yet, this is what is referred to as *good debt*. It's good for a number of reasons, but we're just going to touch on the top three.

First, this kind of debt provides you with an immediate army of soldiers so that you won't be required to go through life on your own. In *Joyful Wealth*, we discussed the value of time and how limited it really is. No one knows how much or how little they have left, so how can we afford to wait for a better time to start? And why would we want to spend all the time we do have trying to build our own army singlehandedly?

---

[16] Erica Alini, "Over Half of Canadians Are $200 or Less Away from Not Being Able to Pay Bills," *Global News*. October 12, 2017 (https://globalnews.ca/news/3434447/over-half-of-canadians-are-200-or-less-away-from-not-being-able-to-pay-bills/).

The second reason also relates to time. How much further will your army expand if you begin today rather than waiting twenty years? Let's reference the penny versus million dollar gift again. If the first cent doubles in value every day for thirty days, it won't have any fighting power compared to the million dollars until the twenty-fifth day. The doubling power of those next five to six days really illustrates the effects of compounding interest for patient investors.

Borrowing someone else's army is essentially like taking advantage of the powerful doubling penny but starting out with the million dollar gift on day one rather than one cent. Can you imagine what that scenario would look like? The penny will be worth millions before the thirtieth day, so what would the million dollars be worth if you started there instead? Do you think you would gain enough wealth to pay the interest and perhaps earn a small commission along the way? Of course you would, and all the while you'd be developing your own army so that you could return the original army to its rightful owner, and still have a significant force left fighting for you into the future. Yes, that would be good debt indeed.

The final reason is that the government pays you to have it. Debt is considered good if it provides you with an opportunity to reduce your income tax relative to the cost of borrowing.

How do good debt tax deductions work?

Imagine that you borrowed $100,000 to invest. The government would consider the cost of borrowing that army a tax-deductible expense. For illustration purposes, say that the interest payment on such a loan equates to $400 per month. When you borrow to invest, however, in addition to interest, you need to consider other costs, such as legal fees, appraisals, loan origination fees, and renewal fees. These can all be deducted.

The government will provide you with a tax credit equal to the same percentage they deduct from your personal income. If you're in a forty percent income tax bracket, then subtract forty percent from $400—in this case, $160 will be given back to you by way of a tax credit.

You may not get very excited about that straight away, but look at what that means over the course of the loan. Twelve months of interest on this one loan could garnish you a tax credit of almost $2,000. That $2,000 may represent the foundation of your very own army, and it's really nothing more than a by-product of borrowing someone else's army, even if the army you borrow doesn't succeed on the battlefield.

If you're a pictures and numbers person, like me, these words may seem a little too complicated to keep track of. When we put some actual figures to these words, I think the benefits of good debt will become glaringly obvious.

When you borrow someone else's $100,000 to go to battle, there's a strong chance you will have to put, as they say, some skin in the game. Five to ten percent down is most common for people just starting out. So to make it most realistic, let's suggest you put up $10,000 to get this army going. Because of your tax deduction on the cost of borrowing, you'll get a $2,000 income tax credit, which represents a twenty percent return right out of the gate.

Note that we haven't accounted for all the additional costs we previously mentioned. Does that catch your attention?

Now, what if this newly formed financial force were to hit the battlefield and grow a conservative seven percent that first year? A seven percent growth on a $110,000 base investment would be an increase of $7,700. How does this make your $10,000 initial investment look now? Remember, you essentially deployed ten thousand soldiers to get this battle started. By the end of year one, because you were in a forty percent personal income tax bracket and your investment grew by seven percent, the number of soldiers you now own has almost doubled. You would now own the ten thousand you started with, plus two thousand more from the government, plus 7,700 from the growth of the investment.

Depending on the variables involved, it's realistic to believe you could end up with twenty thousand soldiers after your first year. Wouldn't you be excited to see what happens in year two, three, ten, or even twenty? That, my friend, is what joyful finances is really about. If you aren't excited about your financial future and that of your army, go back to the drawing board and work on a new game plan to win the next battle. Too many people concede before reaching the finish line, not realizing how close they were to success.

Don't call in all your troops and just watch them parish. Be a good commander: organize, strategize, and develop a plan that can take full advantage of the three reasons to take on good debt. Once prepared, go get some good debt, lead it into battle, and let someone else's army do most of your fighting for you.

Before we move on, here's a lesson from the rich. What they've learned is that they can invest their income into assets (anything that puts money in their pocket) and allow those assets to pay for the cost of liabilities (things that take money out of their pocket).

Can you imagine what it would be like to own a brand-new car and never have to make a payment on it personally because you own an asset that makes the payments for you? How about your dream house? A boat perhaps? Maybe you like to travel. How enjoyable would a first-class trip to Bora Bora be if someone, or something, else paid for it?

Now, of course there's two sides to every coin. Whereas good debt works for you, bad debt works against you. Later in this book, I'll share some strategies my wife and I have found tremendously effective tactics in destroying bad debt. These techniques can be used to launch an assault to reduce, shift, or completely eliminate your bad debt—starting today.

But not all debt is equal, nor is all debt bad. If debt were completely negative all the time, and there were never advantages to having debt, then debt reduction strategies would be an easy topic to explain. In fact, that book would include just one page, and on it would be printed something like this: *Use every available dollar you have and knock down your debt.* End of book.

I assure you there's a lot more to consider about debt reduction than just how fast it can be eliminated. In fact, if you're entirely focused on retiring all the debts you currently carry, you're likely doing it at the cost of a wealthy financial future. Nearly every account I've read of people gaining significant wealth includes the assistance of good debt.

To be clear, owing $800 to the cell phone company for four years certainly isn't the kind of debt I'm referring to here. Neither is the debt you owe to Vinny, from that time when he bailed you out of a tight spot. Those are bad debts, and your life is going to have much more joy when you take responsibility and pay them out.

You may be thinking the debt to the cell phone company will disappear in a couple of years, when they get tired of chasing you. Or maybe Vinny will forget about that favour; after all, it was such a long time ago.

But here's the thing: the phone company has certainly registered your debt with the credit bureau, and in Chapter Three we discussed the importance of having your credit in order.

As for Vinny? Well, he may not mention it each time he sees you, but trust me—he hasn't forgotten. He knows exactly what you've done, and it crosses his mind more often than you imagine. No one likes to help someone out financially only to have their good intentions and hard-earned money disrespected by lack of repayment.

If you wish to pursue a life of joy, you must honour those who have helped you along the way.

It Started with Moses

When God provided Moses the Ten Commandments, the eighth commandment said, *"Thou shalt not steal"* (Exodus 20:15, KJV). So these are not new principles I'm sharing with you.

If you still think the phone company won't care whether you pay them back, you've missed the point. Paying your debts isn't about the person who lent you the money in the first place, it's about you. This book is about *your* joyful financial future, not theirs.

You're absolutely right—that massive corporation that generated $4 billion in revenue last year likely won't feel a thing if you don't pay them, but you will.

Put another way, how would it make you feel to be known as a thief? Whether it's a $5 item from a big box store or $800 worth of service you've taken and not paid for, is there a qualifying value that determines whether you're a thief or not? Or is stealing simply stealing?

Here's the best thing about this revelation: if you owe money to a business, such as the phone company, it's not too late to pay them back. That's right. Who cares if you've switched providers three years ago and the last time you talked to the accounts receivable department of your old phone carrier was when you hung up on them because they made you so mad. The bottom line is that you still have a debt and they'd likely be willing to accept your payment.

How much joy would you experience if you could go back and return everything you'd ever stolen? Doing this is life-changing, which I know from personal experience! If you've ever thought of calling a past debtor but wondered how you would even begin such a conversation, try this:

> Hi, my name is _____. I used to be a customer of yours and when I left ____ years ago, I had an unpaid balance of $____. It was wrong of me to leave it outstanding as long as I have, but I would like to commit to retiring that debt in full, either by making a payment today or setting up a monthly payment plan until it's gone. Is there someone who can help me with that please?

The weight on your shoulders will begin to lift as you do this, replacing it with joy. And isn't it true that although you may have taken something, if you return it then you've essentially borrowed the item, not stolen it? Guess what, my friend? You are not a thief! How great is that?

On one occasion, the person answering the phone directed me to the manager because my account had been locked due to inactivity and she was unable to pull up the details. When the manager got on the phone and was able to pull up the details, she made me the following offer:

Mr. Bondy, I can see that you were a good standing client for a long time. I'm sorry that you fell into difficult circumstances and appreciate that you are reaching out to us today to clear your account. Not many ever do. Since you're willing to make a payment today, we will accept fifty percent of what your outstanding balance was, and I will change the status of your file in our system to preferred client. If you ever decide to return to our company, we would be very pleased to do business with you again. Is there anything else I can help you with today?

I encourage you to pay the man, pay the company, pay the lender… just pay your debt, regardless of what your perception of their financial position is. Pay what you owe and avoid living the life of a thief.

Back to Moses for a moment. The fifth commandment said, *"Honour thy father and thy mother…"* (Exodus 20:12, KJV)

Mom and Dad deserve to be honoured for the commitment they make in being the best parents they can. That doesn't mean they need to be perfect, or that they aren't going to make mistakes along the way. It means that because they were committed to raising you as a child, you should honour that.

Throughout every stage of life, I hope you've had people to look up to. It may not be a biological parent. Perhaps it's a relationship counsellor, a career coach, an investment advisor, or a spiritual leader. I've been blessed with a multitude of counsellors in my life. Not all were professional counsellors, though, and in many cases some of our best counsellors have been people with more experience than me in a given field, at a given time. These can develop into mentoring relationships.

If you've ever had a relationship of this nature, be it one that you've paid for or one that has developed from a friendship, you would likely agree that this person takes on a parental role. You become comfortable asking them for their opinion or advice. They provide honest feedback because they know what's best for you. They stand beside you even when you make mistakes. And when you succeed, you anxiously anticipate sharing your progress with them because you know they'll be equally excited to share in your victories.

And yes, sometimes they may even extend a hand to financially help you through something you're going through. How could you consider not paying that person back in full and expecting to have a joyful life in the future? You can't!

Honouring your father and mother isn't just an ageless commandment. It applies to all those people who have parented you along the path of life.

At many points in my life, I have experienced financial ups and downs. As a business owner since my teenage years, job security hasn't been a goal of mine. I spent the first thirty years of my life trying to figure out how to make it on my own, turning lemons into lemonade.

There are certainly many benefits that accompany successful business ownership, and there are a few drawbacks as well. The most difficult one that consistently challenged me was cashflow. Sure, on paper Megan and I had all kinds of revenue. One person in our office was almost completely dedicated to producing invoices for the work everyone on the various teams was doing. I learned very quickly, however, that just because we sent out an invoice didn't mean we would get paid immediately. And when payment did come, it was often required to be put towards payroll, the fuel account balance, the equipment loans, or a multitude of other expenses.

As an aggressive business builder, it was my personal mandate to capitalize on as many lucrative opportunities as possible. I simply wouldn't allow a lack of money to be the reason we didn't do something. I borrowed money from every imaginable source, and if not for the wise counsel of a financial mentor that accompanied me to a specific meeting, that list would have included some very dangerous people as well.

"Ryan, unless you want to end up at the bottom of the river wearing cement boots, you are not going to borrow from this guy," my mentor said to me very sternly one day as we walked away from a prospective lender's office.

My excitement was squashed, but at least I'm still here to share the memory.

I remember facing collective debt that exceeded seven figures. When the numbers were presented to me on paper, I felt anything but joyful. Taking a long and very dry swallow, I sat at my desk and wondered how I would ever get out of it.

In full transparency, I simply didn't have enough income to meet all my obligations. Payroll came around every fourteen days whether I wanted it to or not, and it seemed we were surviving just to meet payroll. After that, if there was anything left, we would play roulette with the massive list of invoices competing for our attention.

But I really don't think we were much different than other businesses. In time, we learned to manage our finances better and stabilize our business activity so the extreme highs and lows were less severe.

I must share, though, that every single one of the vendors we owed got paid in full. To this day, we enjoy wonderful working relationships with every one of them.

Because of the honour I directed toward a small locksmith company by paying them back, they treat me like a top-notch business partner when I walk into their office today. They know that although circumstances prevented me from paying them at first, I very clearly communicated my intentions to pay them in full, and over the next year and a half I consistently gave them everything I could until the debt was retired. Do you know the joy that accompanies such a final payment? The look of appreciation in the business owner's eyes was worth the effort, but knowing that this business could trust me has proven to be an immense source of joy to this day.

This chapter was intended to share with you that there's a lot more to joyful finances than just having a lot of money. Joy is derived from many sources, and it's abundantly available to the person who makes the conscious decision to look for it. Sometimes that will mean putting extra money in your pocket, and other times it will mean taking a little extra out of your pocket. Joyful is the person who knows they have a solid financial foundation, and because of that they have the ability to look forward to the future with a sense of anticipation of great things to come.

I want to thank all those authors who unknowingly spoke joy into me through all these years. It hasn't come naturally, or by luck; it takes time and energy, as does anything worth pursuing.

My wish for you as we continue is that you embrace the journey that is your financial path. Success is more than just a destination in life. Those who experience daily joy along the way have already reached success, regardless of how far away the destination appears.

Enjoy your journey toward joyful finances and you, too, will be successful from this day forward. Congratulations on taking the necessary steps to create the financial future you have been dreaming of. Now go get it!

12

For you are my hiding place; you protect me from trouble. You
surround me with songs of victory.
(Psalm 32:7, NLT)

Despite being in business for thirty years and managing millions of dollars' worth of investments and real estate, the area of financial management that has always confused me most is insurance. How much should you have? Of what kind? When is it needed? When do you collect? Where should you get it from? Is it all the same? These sorts of questions plagued me for more than two decades.

Thankfully, we have a very patient and understanding insurance broker who handles our insurance needs, and he and my wife have managed the majority of these issues.

However, I made the decision that if I was going to write a book about financial joy, then it had to include some clear ideas regarding the different kinds of insurance products available. The importance of insurance, a tool specifically designed to protect the very soldiers we spend our entire lives trying to amass, cannot be overlooked.

In consultation with some insurance professionals, we have set out to clear up the fogginess regarding insurance, including its most misunderstood elements. As with any other aspect of your financial position, it's key to have good partnerships you can rely on and trust, people who know the ins and outs of an industry and can apply what is best for you to your specific needs without becoming crippled by the seemingly unlimited number of options available to you. Just as a lawyer knows the law, an accountant knows the numbers, or a realtor knows the local market, a good insurance agent is key to securing the kind of protection that will permit you to confidently charge into the future without fear of a surprise attack. In

> Just as a lawyer knows the law, an accountant knows the numbers, or a realtor knows the local market, a good insurance agent is key...

the event you do run into something unexpected, the proper coverage will mitigate the damage to your platoon and even nurse them back to health. That peace of mind is why insurance has become such a significant component in creating a joyful financial future for yourself.

Throughout this chapter, we're going to review various kinds of personal and professional products that have been designed to protect you as an individual, as a family, and even as a small company.

Aside from the dry disclaimer, there's a much more serious disclaimer I need to set forward: I'm certainly not an insurance agent, nor am I suggesting you purchase any one of the following products based on what I say about it. Professional advice in this field should come from an active licensed agent in the business who understands your specific needs and goals.

We will begin with some personal coverage and work through the types of scenarios where these products may prove to be most beneficial.

Personal Coverages

So how do we position ourselves to best face risk in our lives? It has been explained to me like this: "In life, we can either transfer, reduce, retain, or avoid risk." To further explain each of these positions, definitions are helpful.

Transfer risk. You can transfer your personal risk to an insurance carrier for a predetermined cost (or premium) to protect you against financial loss. Car insurance, for instance, would be an example of a transfer of risk.

Reduce risk. You may decide to insure your spouse in case they lose income. Another example is encouraging your partner to exercise and eat a healthy diet to reduce risks.

Retain risk. Some things are not insurable at all, such as one's personal reputation.

Avoid risk. If you don't want to risk having an accident while driving a car, one solution would be to not own a car.

In science classes, we are taught that for every action, there is an equal but opposite reaction. Does that lesson ring any bells for you? In this context, it means that to avoid exposure to risk, you can refrain from doing things in life. The more you do, however, the more risk you expose yourself to.

Your need for protection, therefore, is directly related to how close you get to the frontline. If you want to be the kind of general who leads your troops from the solitude of a confined bunker, you likely aren't going to be exposed to much risk in life. On the other hand, if you happen to be a more hands-on leader, then let's face it: you'll require some serious protection.

The famous Muhammad Ali had an often-expressed mantra: "He who is not courageous enough to take risks will accomplish nothing in life." I would venture to believe that you're holding this book right now because you're a hands-on type of leader who yearns to take control of your financial battle.

There are coverages for people like you. They're called life insurance policies.

Life Insurance

In simple terms, life insurance is a sum of money made available to a person after a period of time, or to their family after they die, in exchange for regular payments. We'll now review different products and discuss the various terms associated with each.

Term life insurance. This type of insurance is a specific amount of coverage designed to protect the policyholder for a predetermined period of time. That is to say, should one acquire this protection at the age of twenty-five and agree to pay the policy until they turn sixty-five, the coverage would expire on their sixty-fifth birthday.

During this forty-year period, the policyholder is protected. However, if they survive that period and the policy expires, there is no payout, no cash value, and no further coverage.

For that reason, this type of life insurance is the least expensive to purchase. As a young person just starting out in life, if your family had a history of heart disease and your life expectancy was relatively short, this could be a valuable way to affordably protect your future family from the devastation of your untimely death.

Whole life insurance. If you want to acquire a more permanent type of coverage, whole life insurance is an option to consider. One of the advantages to this type of policy is that in addition to a specified amount of coverage, there is also a built-in savings component. With each monthly payment made by the policyholder, a percentage of that payment is directed into an attached savings account. If needed, the policyholder is even entitled to borrow against the cash value of this account. Also, the policy can be surrendered prior to death and cashed in for the full cash value payout. In the event that the policyholder should die, the insurance company will pay the beneficiary the face value of the policy, as well as the cash accumulation that was in the savings account.

Whereas term life insurance is designed to protect the policyholder from death that may occur during a specified period in time, whole life insurance can be used as an investment tool as much as a protection device. It retains some of the value that's been invested into it, and the policyholder can benefit while they're still alive.

Universal life insurance. This is also a type of permanent life insurance with a built-in savings vehicle. The policyholder can overcontribute to this policy and the money in the policy's savings account can be overfunded, tax-free.

Research suggests that this is the more expensive of the life insurance options, but some might argue that the ability to overfund and realize tax-free growth is worth the premium cost.

Thus far, although there is some benefit to be realized by the policyholder while they're alive, the majority of the benefits in these policies are intended to financially protect those left who are left behind.

There are, however, a number of products that will benefit someone while they're alive.

Personal Insurance

In the unfortunate event that someone requires long-term care, becomes disabled, or falls ill to the point of being unable to perform their regular income-generating tasks, the following might be helpful.

Long-term care insurance. This type of specialty coverage provides money for one's care in the event of an accident that prohibits them from performing their regular activities. Generally, the policyholder pays a monthly premium for a monthly payout. The amount of this payout is predetermined at the start of the policy.

Disability insurance. It has been reported that nearly fifteen percent of Canadians have a disability, and one in three Canadians will be disabled for three months or longer before the age of sixty-five. For this reason, many employers will include disability coverage as part of their group insurance plans.

Disability insurance is designed to cover part of a person's income in the event they become disabled, whether at work or otherwise. There is a monthly premium for this coverage, and the payout arrives in a monthly lump sum so that payments will cease in the event that the injured party should recover. There is normally a waiting period before a person can collect these payments after becoming disabled—and this should be clearly spelled out and explained in the terms of the policy.

The value of this benefit is difficult to predetermine, as it is generally paid out as a percentage of the person's lost wage, after factoring in other incomes.

Critical illness insurance. The purpose of critical illness insurance is to help with unexpected expenses that occur because of an illness. These plans typically cover medication, lost income from a disability, optional treatment, etc. It is usually available in a basic package, covering heart attack, stroke, and cancer. If one is so inclined to opt for an enhanced plan, there are up to twenty-five additional illnesses that can also be covered.

The policy offers a single lump sum payout. It then lapses, unless you have a second event rider, in which case it could pay out again for a different condition.

Let's put some real figures behind this so you can better understand how this might look. If you were to purchase a policy that provided $10,000 in the event of a heart attack, once the condition has been paid for it comes off the list. If you had a stroke later in life, the policy would provide the payout allocated to that specific event. You can imagine how expensive it would be to get additional heart attack coverage after you've already made a claim for a prior heart attack. This policy provides a one shot-benefit, so take care of yourself!

In a nutshell, these are a few different insurance products you can purchase to protect yourself and the soldiers you've nurtured.

If your goal is to enjoy joyful finances, would you not agree that it would be good idea to have a little safety net? I've heard it said that jumping out of a plane really isn't that dangerous, provided you have a good parachute. Perhaps these products can be viewed as parachutes; depending on your altitude, the climate, and your personal physique, you need to pick the ones that are right for you. And it may be beneficial to deploy more than one layer of protection.

The goal here is to make you more aware of the products available to you—more aware than I've been most of my life.

More than Personal Coverage

As with any business, the main objective of an insurance provider is to provide a product or service that customers will benefit from. Simultaneously, these companies have to generate an operational profit. To achieve this, they must remain creative.

The above mentioned products are all focused on protecting the policyholder directly. However, there are a lot of other products in the insurance industry that are designed to protect your stuff.

Again, there are more specific products than I can include in this single chapter, particularly as you drill into business coverages, so the purpose here is merely to offer you a glance at some of the more common coverages. It is my personal belief that with the use of some of these products, you may enjoy a more joyful financial future.

Additional Terms

As we begin to look at coverages on real estate, personal property, and business operations, we will be introduced to a few new terms.

Deductible. The deductible is your portion of a claim. This means that in the event of a claim, while a policy may cover the lion's share of the repair or replacement cost, you will be responsible for a shared cost in order to complete the claim. Higher deductibles may or may not make sense for you based on how much money you feel comfortable being able to pay in the event of an incident.

For example, while your auto insurance policy may cover the value of your $10,000 vehicle, in the event of an accident you may be required to pay a deductible of $250 before the claim is paid out. On a policy that protects a $200,000 home, the deductible may be higher, such as $1,000 to $5,000. The premium associated with the coverage will be directly reflective of the deductible amount, thus it is important to evaluate whether it's wise to increase or decrease the deductible in certain situations.

Causes of loss. Basic property insurance policies are written to cover the risks of fire, lightning, explosion, windstorm, hail, smoke, aircraft or vehicle damage, riot or civil commotion, vandalism, or sprinkler leakage. The "broad form" policy adds coverage for water damage, weight of snow, ice, sleet, breakage of glass, and falling objects. The broadest coverage is known as the "all risk form," which covers all causes of loss, except those specifically excluded.

Other Types of Insurance

Personal property insurance (tenant insurance). Probably the most recommended product I've shared with people throughout the years is personal property insurance, which offers an inexpensive opportunity for people to protect their stuff, even if they don't own the building they live in.

This is particularly essential in an environment that may include multiple families living under one roof. While the owner is likely to have protection for the brick and mortar of the building itself, in the event of a fire or flood, the owner's insurance will not cover their residents' contents. Personal property insurance is designed to do just that.

The monthly premium is determined by the value of coverage needed, which is simply calculated by adding the value of the items in your possession. These items could include computers, televisions, furniture, clothing, tools, appliances, toys, and so on.

The specific purpose of this kind of insurance is to ensure that if there's an insured loss, you'll be able to make a claim even if you don't own your home, and if you're not responsible for the cause of loss. For example, your items will be replaced if they're lost in a fire that was started in the unit below you, or in a flood caused by the resident above.

Wouldn't that bring a certain joyful peace of mind, knowing that although you may be exposed to a certain amount of risk, you have a blanket of protection should anything happen?

Real property insurance. If you are the owner of a property, whether it's your primary residence, a commercial building, or a rental unit, real property insurance is meant for you. In the event of an insurable loss, real property is defined as the land and attachments to the land, such as a building. Everything else is considered personal property.

In a similar exercise as the resident, the property owner must determine the replacement value of the entire building, with the assistance of an insurance broker. So in the event of a complete loss, or even just a partial loss, the owner can rest assured that their property is protected, in exchange for a monthly or annual premium.

Mortgage life insurance. Most homeowners are familiar with the concept of a mortgage. Mortgage life insurance is essentially a term policy that is tied to your mortgage. The lending institution becomes the beneficiary in the event that the borrower should pass away.

There is one gleaming downside to these policies. Since the policy benefit is directly related to the balance of the mortgage, the insurance payout amount lowers as the mortgage is paid down, and yet the premiums remain the same.

For example, if Steve were to take out a $100,000 mortgage to purchase his home, and at the time the mortgage was initiated he opted for the available mortgage insurance offered by the lending institution, the cost may be less than $20 per month. Five years later, Steve will have paid off nearly $10,000 and now owe just $90,000 on his mortgage. His premium doesn't change, however. In the event of his untimely death, the policy benefit would only be ninety percent of the original amount.

It has been suggested that mortgage insurance is pricier than a term policy. While the term policy does not reduce in face value, it would appear to be a far better deal.

Small business insurance. There's a lot of variation in terms of insurance protections for business ownership, so my goal here will be to hit on some of the most common ones. The type of coverage you'll need is directly related to the kind of exposure your business may have. It would seem fairly obvious that a go-cart operating business would have a different level of exposure than perhaps a bookkeeping business.

Make no mistake about it, however: every business has some exposure, and insurance products have been created to allow business owners to have peace of mind.

Common types of coverage include buildings, completed additions to covered buildings, outdoor fixtures, HVAC, and permanently installed equipment such as overhead cranes.

On the other hand, business personal property insurance will cover things that the business may own—equipment, furniture, fixtures, stock, etc. Leased equipment can also be covered.

The policy will protect an owner against loss or damage to the personal property of others while in the possession of the business, so long as it relates to the business. For instance, if a vehicle is brought to a mechanic to have work performed, the vehicle will be covered from damage or loss that may occur while in the shop.

In addition to the standard items most businesses would want to insure, there are other coverages that might apply, such as to newly acquired or constructed property, inflationary increases in building value, the removal of debris, limited pollution coverage, certain outdoor property, and the cost to research and reconstruct information for destroyed business records.

If your coverage is on a "broad form," two additional extensions could be added: for property in transit, and for certain water damage claims. The coverage applies to removal of debris, preservation of property, fire department service charges, and pollutant cleanup and removal.

Liability insurance. Any insurance that protects the policyholder from civil responsibilities to outside parties is referred to as liability insurance. This could refer to the general public, users of your product, your customers, etc.

While there are many specialized forms of protection, the most common is the commercial general liability policy, which will pay damages for which you may be responsible by law, such as in the case of an injury or death, or damage to a person's property, which occurs as a result of your business, its products, or the actions of your employees. This type of policy doesn't cover injuries to your employees, nor to damage to property in your control (which may be covered under your property policy).

In addition to providing payment to outside parties, the insurer will also defend you against all lawsuits, even if they're groundless; pay all costs of actions and all interest after judgment; pay the cost of all appeal bonds; and reimburse you for the cost of providing first aid to injured persons.

If the structure of your organization includes directors and officers, there is a product available to protect them as well. This coverage will repay the organization and its directors and officers against claims for wrongful acts that occur as a result of their own decision-making.

Errors and omissions insurance is a type of professional liability insurance that protects companies, workers, and other professionals against claims of inadequate work or negligent actions. This form of protection often covers both court costs and any settlements up to the amount specified by the policy benefit. This kind of liability insurance is generally required for when you provide professional advice or provide a service.

Finally, employees often use other people's vehicles in conjunction with their business. If this applies to you, you could seek out non-owned automobile insurance, which protects you for property damage to other cars, or injuries to other drivers arising out of the negligent actions of the vehicle being used, so long as the use is on behalf of your business.

Specialty coverages. These are designed to protect specific aspects of one's business, such as employee dishonesty and crime, boiler and machinery, extra expense insurance, or business interruption insurance.

What's It All Worth?

This is a bone of my contention when it comes to insurance in general, and it's something I have fought for years to understand.

While property can be valued in several ways, insurers commonly use only two approaches: replacement cost and actual cash value. Replacement cost is how much money would be needed to replace the property. Actual cash value equals the replacement cost minus any accumulated depreciation for age and condition.

With either approach, it's important to determine what the benefit of the policy truly is before you need to make a claim. Otherwise, you risk great disappointment, not only because of your loss but because of the discrepancy between the coverage you thought you had and what your policy actually provides.

Nearly every policy will have a co-insurance clause, which requires one to carry insurance equal to at least a specified percentage of the value of the property (replacement cost or actual cash value). If a loss occurs, and it is shown that the amount of insurance is less than the amount required, the insurer's payment will be reduced.

In any event, in this chapter we've talked about a lot of different kinds of coverage. While you may not require them all—and there are more available than the ones I've mentioned, to be sure—the important takeaway is that because you work so hard to acquire and train your soldiers, it's crucial that you protect them before you send them into battle.

13

Backing Your Troops

Wealth from get-rich-quick schemes quickly disappears; wealth
from hard work grows over time.
(Proverbs 13:11, NLT)

As we discussed in the earlier chapter about different types of investments, one of the greatest advantages we have is leverage—specifically in the real estate market. Because real estate has a more universal understanding of value, it's generally much easier to obtain financial assistance when acquiring property. The questions then become, how much can you borrow and where will you borrow it from?

What follows are some helpful hints about where you can turn if you find a deal but realize there's a shortfall in your bank account and you can't pay cash in full.

It should be noted that some investors will qualify for financing opportunities related to certain types of paper investments, but since those opportunities are limited to a small percentage of investors we'll focus on real estate acquisitions specifically.

How Much Can You Borrow?

To begin to answer this question, we must have a willingness to go into debt. In some circles, debt is a very negative four-letter word. To a sophisticated investor who understands their market and the benefits of leverage, debt is welcomed with the understanding that there's a significant difference between good and bad debt.

If you're comfortable owing someone $100,000, $200,000, or even $1,000,000, then you're ready to proceed.

If the immediate thought of borrowing has you wiggling in your chair right now, you should complete the following exercise to adjust your inner beliefs as they relate to borrowing and investing before going any further.

To help set your mind at ease, here's a simple scenario to get you thinking about debt more like an investor, and less like someone who thinks they need to borrow because they don't have enough money. Sure, it may be true that you don't have enough money at the moment, but investors with more money than you and me still borrow money to invest all the time.

And here's why.

Lauren is a hard-working woman. She's been working her profession for a long time, and along the way she's built up the trust of a long-time client. This client, Greg, is a very intelligent person who likes to trade items he finds in yard sales and sell them online.

One day, Greg tells Lauren that he's extremely busy and cannot figure out how to pick up and deliver an item he purchased and sold to someone else. As kind as she is, Lauren offers to handle the pickup and delivery, as a favour, because Greg has been such a good client for so long.

Greg makes her a deal. "Lauren, I'll tell you what—I've already paid for the item, so I'll let the seller know you're picking it up for me. When you deliver it to the new owner, she'll pay you $55. I was willing to accept $45 for the item when I listed it for sale, so you keep the $10 and put it toward your fuel cost."

Do you think Lauren had any problem borrowing $45 from her client to make this transaction? The answer is, of course not. In fact, she doesn't even think of it as borrowing, and neither would most people.

Why is that? Lauren took possession of something that someone else had paid for, and then she sold it to someone else for a profit which she benefited from. At that time, she paid back the loan and parted with her proceeds. All parties were pleased when the transaction was complete.

Whether she thinks about it or not, Lauren was perfectly comfortable accepting a $45 loan from Greg the moment she offered to complete the transaction for him.

If you struggled to see this as an example of a loan transaction, don't be surprised. The reason it's difficult to see at first glance is due to the amount being borrowed and the short length of the loan. In industry, this would be considered a microloan.

Let's put it another way. If you had to borrow $40 from a friend at a restaurant because the debit machine was down and you hadn't come with enough cash, would it bother you until you paid them back the next time you saw them? Not likely.

So at what point does a little IOU become a debt that you begin to feel uncomfortable about? That's the position you have to identify for yourself. There is no right or wrong answer, and with age, experience, and wisdom, your answer will likely change with time.

Be honest with yourself. If someone offered to lend you $20,000 that needed to be paid back on reasonable terms, over the next two years, would you lose sleep over that debt? How about $100,000 over the next ten years? Keep increasing the number, thinking about how you would feel knowing that you had this outstanding amount due at some point.

Take an honest look at what you would feel about each number until you reach the point where you realize you simply couldn't sleep at night because you would be overcome with worry. Once you reach that point, I would suggest that you reduce the amount by about thirty percent and make that your maximum comfort level for borrowing.

How Much Will Someone Lend You?

Let's get creative. There are different types of lenders out there, and where real estate is concerned, those lenders are generally categorized as traditional lenders or private lenders.

Private lenders. These are very creative people who are often much more flexible than traditional lenders. However, they do cost more to utilize. They'll lend up to as much as one hundred percent of the project cost, including property acquisition and improvement costs. They tend to be more aggressive when it comes to real estate lending than a traditional lender because they know the industry they're lending in. Oftentimes they're real estate owners themselves.

Generally, private lenders are high-income earners in a community, possibly an individual investor or a group of investors who know the marketplace and understand the risks. This is often referred to as *creative financing*, because the breadth of terms and conditions is limitless.

For example, you may approach a private lender and create a deal that looks something like this.

Ivan the investor: "So I'd like to purchase a rental property and I have a decent paying job, but I'm having a difficult time saving up enough money to please the banks. This is what I have so far—$5,000 in cash, a four-year-old car that's almost paid for, a twenty-two-foot boat, some mutual funds, and a really great baseball card collection, probably worth $3,500 to $4,000. What I need is $100,000 to purchase the property, and then it will carry itself, as the current tenants are paying $1,295 plus utilities on a two-year lease."

Lenny the lender: "Sounds like a good opportunity. Here's what I'm going to offer you. I'll lend you $95,000 at ten percent annual interest, for two years. For the first twelve months, I'll let you pay interest-only payments, which will be $791. Let's round that off to $800. The second year, you can pay $1,000 per month and the balance will be due in full at the end of the twenty-fourth month. In the event that you're unable to meet any of your payment obligations, we'll take ownership of the property. We'll place a lien on your boat and car during this time, and I'd like to hold your baseball card collection as collateral until the loan is repaid."

You may be thinking this is ridiculous, that no one would ever negotiate terms and conditions like those listed above, but that's what creative financing is all about. The more creative you are, the more likely you are to find the money you need to make a deal happen.

This is why while some believe that it takes money to make money, others realize that this is only partially true; the complete truth is that when you think creatively, you'll find the money you need to make the money you want. But you certainly don't need to have it yourself. Many millionaires become millionaires because they were incredibly creative, not because they came from money or saved it up for a really long time.

Traditional lenders. Getting started, it's easier for most beginning investors to use traditional financing, and there are several reasons for this. First, it is much easier to find. Second, it is much less expensive to use. Third, there's much less work required of the borrower.

Whether you see an advertisement on television or a billboard on the side of the road, banks and credit unions are constantly looking for ways to lend money. We've already discussed the reason that lending is so important to banks, but this is a great time to connect the dots if you haven't already done so; this is where an investor begins to understand their value to the bank.

I frequently hear people say, "Oh, I can't get a mortgage. I have nothing to offer the bank." What they're saying is that they have a very limited understanding of how the lending process really works. You see, they have value to the bank the moment they walk through the doors.

To understand this better, we have to go back to our discussion about assets and liabilities.

If you recall, we agreed that if you had a mortgage on your home, your home would be an asset for the bank, by way of interest. Because you borrowed money from them, the house becomes their asset, because the interest is a revenue stream.

So when you walk into a bank looking for a mortgage, you're essentially telling them, "Mr. Bank, I want to increase your income today. Are you interested in working with me on a real estate deal?" This is often all it takes to get the banker's attention.

For instance, imagine if Harry the house hunter walked into the bank and introduced himself to the same banker we just met above. He walks in a little shy and doubts he's going to qualify, but his friend encouraged him to come to the bank to find out if they would do anything for him.

"Hi," Harry says to the banker. "I'd like to buy a house, but I don't have any money. I was told you might lend me some if I came in here and asked. I've never been to a bank before, so I thought I would come down and see if you could buy me a house please."

Does Harry stand a chance with an approach like this? Of course not. Sadly, many have such little understanding of how banking systems work that they think it's an entirely one-sided relationship whereby the bank does all the providing and the client does all the paying.

It's not like that at all. The bank needs clients to borrow money in order to generate income. With a proper understanding of how the system works, a win-win loan can be acquired with very little effort on the borrower's part, aside from providing some personal information and verified income sources. The process is virtually the same whether you're asking for a $50,000 mortgage or a $5,000,000 mortgage. And in both cases, the borrower represents a potential asset to the bank; they should reflect that from the moment they walk into the branch to introduce themselves.

Difference Between Banks and Credit Unions

Today's students are blessed with opportunities to experiment with job placements while they're still in high school, as a way to identify future career paths and the necessary educational path to get there.

In my senior year, I was granted such an opportunity. For one semester, I stood behind the teller of a Royal Bank of Canada (RBC) branch in Belle River, Ontario. I learned much from that experience, and to this day I'm still an active client of that organization.

Through the world of investing, I was introduced to several other major Canadian banking institutions, such as CIBC, Toronto Dominion Bank, and Scotia Bank. When my wife and I began investing in the United States, I made it my mandate to meet with several of the major banks in the U.S. as well, such as Chase, CitiBank, and Bank of America. What I learned from all these introductions is that all banks are not created equal. In other words, when it comes to banking, one size does not fit all.

> ...when it comes to banking, one size does not fit all.

Let me explain, starting with the RBC here in Canada. As a national brand bank, this institution is exactly what you would expect. From the look and layout of their individual branches, to the terms and conditions that apply to their products, each RBC one visits in Canada is very much the same—much the same way that a McDonald's hamburger served in Windsor, Ontario is similar to a McDonald's hamburger served in Regina, Saskatchewan.

When you apply for a loan at an institution such as this, there is very little creativity involved in the application or product provision area. RBC offers certain products, and in order to qualify for them you must meet certain criteria from a checklist. Fail to meet the required checks and you will be declined.

It is possible to outgrow the abilities of a single bank, as we came to learn not long after getting our investment career going. As many banks do, RBC informed us that the maximum number of mortgages they are permitted to extend to one investor, regardless of the cumulative total borrowed, was four. To protect the bank, understandably, they limit an investor's borrowing to four separate mortgage products, such that in the event of a catastrophic loss to the investor, the bank's exposure would be limited.

That is completely understandable, but I struggled with the idea that the dollar value of the mortgage balances was not part of the equation. For instance, if you start investing with a single-family two-bedroom home, which you purchase for $100,000, and put $10,000 down, you require a $90,000 mortgage. Perhaps you do this three additional times in the forthcoming years.

And when you approach the bank to purchase the fifth property, you are denied. They don't consider the fact that you've reduced the principal on the first four mortgages already, or that you now have additional income from the four properties that may add up to more than your earned income. No, because when you deal with a traditional bank, they aren't very flexible when it comes to terms and conditions.

Furthermore, although the total value of your four mortgages may only equate to a grand total debt of $400,000, you would still be denied for the fifth house. It has been suggested to me by various bankers that in order to get another mortgage, I would have to sell one of the existing properties and then purchase another.

However, a preferred option would be to visit an alternative lending institution. Remember, the person doing the borrowing is an asset to the bank, so investors are welcomed at nearly every leading institution out there.

It was this very situation that prompted me to leave RBC, while still using their services, to employ the assistance of other banks to finance additional projects.

Now, if you sit with me for any period of time, you'll likely discover that I have several reservations about the benefits of unions in today's society.

That is, unless you're referring to credit unions.

In recent years, I've come to love these smaller, more personalized, member-owned financial institutions. If you haven't had the pleasure of visiting a local credit union, I strongly urge you to go down and just say hello. Introduce yourself as a stranger to their banking philosophy or business model and ask them to explain what makes them different from a standard model bank. I believe you will find that they take a much more personalized approach. These facilities are owned by the members—a more friendly reference than clients—and proceeds are paid back to those members. Members also have voting rights on various affairs concerning the operation of the credit union, which ensures that they're more informed and involved.

In Canada, credit unions are much smaller than the major national banks and have really only entered the marketplace in force since 2012. While RBC, established in 1864, may operate more than a thousand branches throughout the country, a credit union may have fewer than five branches operating in a specific city or county.

As you can imagine, when you're neither the first to market nor the largest player in the market, you must be incredibly competitive if you are to gain any market share. This is exactly what attracts investors to work with credit unions. I'll demonstrate this using a very specific example of a deal that was presented to both a national brand bank and to a local credit union.

When Peter went to the bank with a very unique opportunity to purchase a property he and his wife were convinced had been developed just for them, they knew there were going to be some challenges getting a mortgage approved. Although they had impeccable credit and plenty of income, the property had some special circumstances they knew the bank would need to consider. It was unique in that it included both a personal residence and a twelve-unit apartment building.

With a quick call to the bank, Peter was immediately recognized by voice and informed that if they wanted a mortgage they would need a thirty-five percent down-payment on a commercial mortgage product—which is a kind way of saying, "We'll lend you the money at a higher rate than people who borrow money to buy a residential home."

But that was a problem for Peter, because a significant percentage of the property included a primary residence, so why the commercial mortgage if he and his wife intended to live on the property? The answer is simple: the bank had used their checklist, and the boxes that got checked indicated that it was primarily a commercial property. Therefore he needed commercial funding, period.

"All right," Peter said. "But because this is going to be my primary residence, can I put a home equity line of credit (HELOC) against the equity in the home portion so that we can access those funds as the mortgage balance is reduced?"

"No, sir," said the person on the other end of the line. "We do not offer HELOCs on commercial properties."

Disappointed but still interested in the property of a lifetime, Peter phoned up the local credit union he had a relatively young relationship with. They certainly hadn't completed nearly as many transactions together, but the consultant on the other end of the phone immediately thanked Peter for his call and suggested a few options for him to consider.

This is evidence of a hungry business operator.

"Peter, here's what I think we can do for you on a deal like this," said the consultant. "First, we'll have to determine what the value of the commercial portion of the property is versus the residential portion. We can then offer you an eighty-five percent loan-to-value mortgage on the residential, and a sixty-five percent mortgage on the commercial side, possibly even seventy-five given that we know you'll be living on the property, which reduces the overall risk involved. Although there will be two separate loans on the property, we'll blend them for you so you have one easy payment. If you're interested in accessing the equity on the home portion, we can also set up a HELOC against the home side, so that would be a third product registered to the property. Does that sound like what you're after?"

He nearly shouted in disbelief, *Heck yes! That's exactly what I'm after.*

Of course, in order to qualify for funding from a credit union, a borrower will have to undergo various applications, pay fees, and take care of all the things the major banks require as well, so there is still a certain level of formality to the process.

What Peter learned during this investigation, however, is that credit unions appear to have much more flexibility than big banks.

With the limited experience I have with the various banks operating in the United States, it's my impression that because the vast majority of them are similar in size to most Canadian credit unions, the business model is similar. There are a few major banks in Canada that also operate south of the border, offering their clients near seamless cross-border banking abilities.

Sadly, it should be noted that, as a foreigner, unless you have an international tax identification number, or a social security number, it is nearly impossible to borrow any amount of money from a U.S. financial institution. While that seemed to be the general response I received while looking to purchase properties throughout the real estate drought of 2008 and 2009, because U.S. banks operate more like Canadian credit unions I was able to meet consultants who were on board with my investment strategy.

So if you were wondering where to go to get your project financed, you now have three very different sources to consider—national banks, credit unions, and private lenders. I would recommend that you start by approaching a local credit union and national bank at the same time, to see if they would be interested in what you're working on.

If neither of those options meet your needs, there are private lenders available to you in nearly any market you can think of. Be reminded that while private lenders are generally much more flexible, they are typically more expensive to use. There are times, however, when it's more important to get the money you need to secure a deal than it is to worry about a three- or four-percent interest rate.

All three of these sources have proven to be incredibly valuable assets to me and my wife during our investment career.

My last piece of advice regarding borrowing is to introduce yourself to lenders before you need any money. Get to know them, and let them get to know you. When the time comes for you to ask for funding, they'll be much more likely to lend to you with favourable terms if they feel comfortable with who you are and know about the project you're proposing for them to finance.

Paul's Story

To close this chapter, I'd like to share a financing story. It's particularly interesting because people thought, at the time that the deal was being put together, that the buyer was naive and making poor borrowing decisions.

Paul was a relatively young investor. With a few single-family homes in his portfolio already, he wanted to find something bigger that would put a little more money in his pocket each month.

While shopping, Paul came across a great duplex that also had a huge garage that could be rented separately for extra money. The owners knew it was a great property, so the asking price was a little higher than Paul wanted to pay, but he knew this was a good opportunity given the three rentable spaces.

Paul didn't have a lot of money to put down, because of the three single-family homes he already owned, so he was looking for creative ways to come up with a down-payment. As he discussed with his banker how he could go about it, the banker shared that Paul could get a cashback mortgage that would return to him seven percent of his borrowed amount on closing. What this means is that for each $100,000 Paul borrowed, he would get a cheque for $7,000 back on the day of closing.

With interest rates at the time being as low as 3.5 percent, Paul's friends laughed at him when he shared that the interest rate on his new mortgage was fixed at 9.9 percent for three years.

Paul knew he could use a credit line to come up with the down-payment he needed to secure the property, which was less than $15,000. With a little more than $9,000 coming back to him when the mortgage closed, Paul had to think of something else he could do to come up with the remainder of the down-payment.

When the idea hit him, he first thought to himself, *Nah. The seller would never go for it.*

But after some consideration, he pitched the following idea. Paul proposed to purchase the property for $2,000 more than asking price (something that was unheard of at the time, although in today's market is common practice), as long as the seller provide to Paul the equivalent of three months' rent as a guarantee. Each month Paul collected rent from his tenants, he then returned that money to the seller.

Additionally, Paul requested a ninety-day closing period for the sale. It was a little longer than the seller wanted, but Paul was hopeful he would go for it.

Once the offer was accepted, Paul would be given the opportunity to rent out the garage to new tenants immediately and collect the new rent until closing.

Despite some obvious issues, Paul knew he had nothing to lose by making the proposal. In the end, the seller grew to like Paul's creative thinking and trusted that Paul's motive was to acquire the property and take care of it. The deal was made with the following conditions:

- Paul agreed on a final purchase price of $145,000.
- Paul put down a down-payment of $14,500 and mortgaged the balance of $130,500.
- Paul paid $2,000 more than asking.
- Paul rented out the garage for $500/month, collecting first and last month's rent, and two additional months' rent before closing, for a total of $2,000.
- Paul was provided a three-month guarantee on the two sets of tenants who were already in place, three months at $600 from the upper tenant, and three months at $850 for the lower tenant, for a total cash advance of $4,350.
- Paul received seven percent of his total borrowed funds at closing, for a total of $9,100.
- Paul's monthly mortgage payment, calculated at 9.9 percent interest, was just under $1,200/month.

Would you borrow at 9.9 percent interest? While the going rate on a traditional mortgage may have been less than half what Paul agreed to pay, and although the property he wanted to purchase required a larger down-payment than he had available, Paul's ability to create opportunities allowed him to purchase the property against the odds.

The question remains, however: was it a good deal or did he overpay for something that was going to cost him more money than it should have? It would be understandable, given the initial review of the circumstances, for Paul to walk away and look for something more affordable, right?

Here's what did happen.

When Paul realized he needed to come up with approximately $14,500 for the down-payment, he knew he could borrow it from either his credit line or his credit cards. He also knew he wouldn't be able to afford the monthly payments on that new balance as well as on the new mortgage he would be getting, so he figured that he needed to come up with a way to pay back the $14,500 before the first payment came due.

By negotiating with the bank, he managed to get a mortgage product that would give him money back straight away. On the day the deal closed, Paul deposited $9,100 into his account. That was a good start. Now he only had to come up with an additional $5,000 to make the deal work.

By offering the seller even more money than he was asking, Paul incentivized him to work with him, and although that cost Paul $2,000 more in the long run, look at what it got him in return. The garage that had previously been vacant was rented immediately and Paul was able to put an additional $2,000 in his pocket prior to the sale's close—an amount equal to the additional money he'd offered the seller—and he was able to convince the seller to put up three months' worth of rent in advance based on the fact that the seller insisted these were good tenants who had never presented any problems. That put an additional $4,350 in Paul's pocket on the day of closing.

Those three items totalled up to $15,450. In fact, when all the funds hit their final destination on that day of closing, Paul ended up with an additional $950 sitting in his contingency account, after making full payment on his credit line balance of $14,500, which he used for the down-payment. His new monthly payment on the property was $1,200, and he had a total rent roll of $1,950 to pay it, leaving him with $750 to make payment on other property-related expenses prior to earning profit.

As you can see, this turned out to be a pretty good deal for Paul, and it required zero of his own dollars to complete. The real power showed up three years later when the initial mortgage matured and Paul was able to renew it at a reduced rate of 3.1 percent for a fixed five-year term. His $1,200 monthly payment was suddenly reduced to just over $550 and his monthly net cashflow immediately doubled to more than $1,300.

It cannot be overstated that you don't need money to make money. The above story is one hundred percent true. People make money every single day even though they have little to nothing to invest when opportunities present themselves. It's not the lack of money that stops people from living a joyful financial lifestyle; it's their lack of willingness to think outside the box and do whatever it takes to get them there.

14

Accelerated Assault

Give to everyone what you owe them: Pay your taxes and
government fees to those who collect them, and give respect and
honor to those who are in authority.
(Romans 13:7, NLT)

Again, I want to be clear that it has never been my primary goal to be debt-free, but rather to obtain joyful finances, which is the ability to look towards the end of the month with excitement about one's financial position. You most certainly don't have to be rich in order to have financial joy. When you get to that point in life where you have more money than month, that's something to get excited about. If you can figure out how to have even $10 more than you need, you may have discovered the formula on how to have $10,000 more than you need.

To achieve this, there are really only two options. You can either increase the amount of money you make, by taking a second job, making an investment, selling something, etc., or you can reduce your expenses, such as lowering you debt load.

We've already discussed various ways to increase your income. In this chapter, we're going to take a closer look at how you can reduce your debt. In the following chapter, we'll also investigate the strategy of reducing your tax expense.

The first debt reduction strategy refers back to previous chapters, where we emphasized the importance of organizing your financial situation. It's simply not effective to jot down your account balance on a napkin every once in a while and expect to have a handle on your circumstances. I would strongly recommend using a spreadsheet like the one we previously illustrated, which ensures that all your income, expenses, and debts are listed accordingly. In order to begin, it's absolutely critical that you understand where you're starting from.

As you implement your strategies, you must also have a way to measure their effectiveness to determine whether you need to make adjustments. Just like that pesky weight scale in the bathroom, or the growth chart etched into the doorframe of your child's bedroom, your ability to see and measure growth will motivate you.

There are a multitude of money management apps you can download to provide you with an organized platform to begin. If you find one of those easier to work with than our own spreadsheet, use it, and keep your figures in front of you on a regular basis. Monitor your activity and celebrate the victories.

Money management generally isn't something most people enjoy or look forward to. This is mainly due to a lack of understanding, or a lack of assistance in creating positive results, and fear that doing so will reveal a budget shortfall. As the old adage says, ignorance is bliss. It's easier to be happy if you don't know exactly how broke you are, right?

Well, we're going to change all that.

Now we'll look at a few ways to reduce your debt, or your interest charges, thus creating some breathing room in your finances.

This is the perfect spot to inject an incredibly important disclaimer: do not reduce your debt or monthly expenses just so you can buy that couch, bed, TV, or car you've really wanted for a long time! Contrary to what you may believe, no, you do not deserve it just because you've figured out a way to finance it. I've seen these kinds of bad decisions land people in terrible financial positions—and the moment they're shown how to escape, they make the same bad decisions all over again.

Say it with me now: "I cannot expect different results unless I start doing something different." If you need to repeat that ten or twenty times before it starts to sink in, go for it. You'll never realize sustainable change until you change the decisions you make.

Take weight loss, for example. It seems like something most people can relate to. Let's say you have a goal to lose ten pounds. First off, you won't get there unless you do something different. It could just be a matter of taking the stairs at work rather than the elevator, but something has to change in order for you to see a different result.

A ten-pound goal is relatively small, so the change may only need to be small. If you want to lose a hundred pounds, the change will need to be much more significant. The key to maintaining the change long-term, however, is consistently implementing the same decision-making that was responsible for creating the change in the first place.

If fifty years of bad decisions have landed you in a place where you feel like you've got a hundred pounds of debt that need to be shed, you may require more significant decision-making changes than just taking the stairs.

As we discuss these strategies, some are likely to seem a little foreign. How foreign they seem is likely directly proportional to the quality of financial decisions you have made up to this point in your life. But before you beat yourself up, know that you aren't alone if you feel like you've made some bad financial decisions. Considering how little education is available to us in terms of wise financial management, the odds have been stacked against you.

There was a time in my own life when I was an ultra-consumer—wild and free, with no regard for financial implications, just optimistically hopeful that somehow my future bliss would work itself out. It's one thing to have hope, but action is required in order to produce results.

If you haven't already mapped out your current position, do that now. List your income, expenses, and debts as accurately as possible. The first step is to have a clear understanding of your starting point.

Starting Out in Life

Freddy was an ambitious fella. However, some would have suggested his eyes were bigger than his bank account. Although no one really pegged Freddy as the university type, when he was accepted into one of the country's finest educational institutes, he packed up his belongings, loaded up his well-used vehicle, and left home for his four-year stay in the campus dorm.

While he was away, he didn't only learn how to position himself for the career of his choice, he was also introduced to the idea that lenders would happily afford you the lifestyle you want right now, so long as you agree to a friendly little payment plan. He realized he could enjoy nicer furniture in his small dorm room for a simple payment of $39 per month.

Semester after semester, Freddy worked hard after hours and studied every minute he could, surprising everyone when he graduated at the top of his class.

By the time graduation came, he was more than ready to leave campus. Freddy now had a $75,000 student loan to return, leaving him with the equivalent of a small mortgage but no home.

Thrilled to have completed his program and hungry to recharge, Freddy and his girlfriend booked a two-week backpacking vacation in Europe before life in the real world began. In order to finance the excursion, he took on a loan with a seventy-two-month payment plan, with payments of $68 per month beginning upon his return.

He came home with a burning passion to find a job in his field, but quickly realized that he would need a more reliable set of wheels to get around. With his new university degree and a record of hard work, the local car dealership found him an amazing honour student discount. With almost nothing down, Freddy stepped into a stylin' new SUV. All he had to pay was $199 per month.

Although Freddy questioned his ability to afford this vehicle, his father was a great encouragement: "I'm so proud of you, son. I've never had a new car in my life, but you deserve it. You've worked so hard to get where you're at. Good for you!"

How could Freddy go wrong? He even had his father's blessing.

Freddy became one of the few from his graduating class to successfully find the job of his dreams directly related to his field of study, but he hadn't really considered that it would be located in one of the most expensive parts of the city. A little shocked by the cost of housing, he decided to split the rent on a house with a friend. Just like that, he had increased his monthly expenses by an additional $500 plus utilities, groceries, insurance, and fuel.

Hard to believe this guy had anything left at the end of the day, isn't it?

Landing in his newly rented home, Freddy thought to himself, *I should go see my friends at the rent-to-own furniture store. The stuff I purchased for my dorm four years ago is getting a little tired. It certainly doesn't fill the space of my new home.* As a preferred client, Freddy was able to quickly secure a new bedroom set, living room set, and a kitchen table and chairs—all for just $145 per month, interest-free for three years. Even though he was still working off the original loan, the lender used his reliable payment history as evidence that he could take on the additional expense.

Now he was all set.

Feeling like a million bucks, Freddy realized he really didn't *look* like a million bucks. After all, he'd been a student all his life, living on campus. His daily wardrobe consisted of some well-worn jeans and his three favourite hoodies.

Armed with a low-interest credit card that had arrived in the mail a few months earlier, Freddy visited the local shops to upgrade his closet. He was a professional now and needed new clothes to match. Within a few hours, he headed home with bags full of pants, shoes, shirts, and even undergarments that were sure to make him feel like the new man he had become.

However, he also had to welcome the $1,725 credit card bill that soon found his mailbox and required minimum monthly payments of $29, exposing the running balance to a whopping 15.99 percent interest rate.[17]

Perhaps you've been tallying up these expenses, realizing that Freddy must have landed a pretty sweet job in order to cover all these monthly payments. While Freddy had landed a sweet job, how much of what he earned could be directed to cover his monthly bills?

Let's do the math:

- $39 for his original dorm room furniture (one more year of payments)
- $625 for his student loan (twelve more years of payments)
- $68 for his backpacking adventure (six more years of payments)
- $199 for his vehicle (three more years of payment)
- $145 for his new furniture (three more years of payments, interest-free)
- $29 minimum monthly payment (twenty-one more years of payments at the 15.99 percent interest rate).

Young Freddy hadn't even started work yet, and his monthly credit commitments had already climbed to more than $1,100 per month. And that didn't include his rent and other living expenses, which added up to another $1,000.

The specifics might not be the same, but most low- and middle-class young people start out in life under similar circumstances. If people start like this, how can they be expected to live a life of true joy when all they've learned is that everything you want is at the tip of your fingers, attached to long payment plans?

I believe we can also agree that the majority of debt Freddy is carrying could be classified as bad debt.

To get out of this, he'll need a plan.

---

[17] By industry standards, this *is* a low-interest credit card.

Three Strategies

Whether you have one hundred troops or ten thousand, there's obvious power in bringing them together.

Perhaps you've had to deal with an ant problem in your home before. You visit that little storage place in the garage and look for the pest control jug. Retrieving it, you realize the container is almost empty. There's only enough to spray the affected area one time, but you know it will take two treatments to be effective.

So what do you do? Do you apply half as much as you should, so that you have enough to cover two treatments, or do you just spray it all one time and hope the problem goes away?

This is a simple illustration, but people spend decades dividing up their limited financial solutions, and ultimately they're ineffective so the problems persist worse than an annoying army of ants.

Strategy #1: Consolidate. Rather than shooting treatment spray in every direction, hoping to hit something, one strategy is to combine all your problems and make a focused attack against them.

Freddy has a school debt payment, a furniture payment, a car payment, a credit card payment, and several other types of payments he's accumulated as a result of seemingly limitless access to credit. And he's short on cash.

Back to the ant infestation example, he has a limited amount of pest control spray. Instead of sprinkling it all over the room, he could decide to drop some honey in the middle of the room and attract all the ants together. This way, his limited amount of spray will stand a better chance of exterminating them.

Nearly any reputable lending facility would consider a consolidated loan for someone like Freddy. He's a hard worker, he demonstrates career ambition, and he's been faithful to make his payments on time, regardless of how much (or how little) they impact his debt load.

The main reason the bank would create a consolidated loan for him is because he came to them with a plan.

Imagine that an army general shows up and asks you for ten thousand of your finest people to fight for him.

"What will they be assigned to do?" you ask.

He replies, "I'm not really sure. I just figured that if I had more troops in front of me, I wouldn't die as quickly."

How seriously would you take this general? It sounds like a suicide mission, not just for the general, but for every troop in his control.

Now, if the general presented a well-considered strategy that included isolating the enemy, hitting a specific target, and advancing with laser-like focus, you may be more inclined to stand behind him.

So what happens when you consolidate?

Freddy's debt is considered bad debt, for the most part, with the exception of his school debt, assuming he is, in fact, working in his field. In that case, his education could be considered an investment, and his accountant could determine that the interest on the loan is tax-deductible. Should that be the case, he would want to keep his student loan (good debt) separate from the rest (bad debt).

At the bank, Freddy seeks to acquire a consolidation loan with an interest rate equal to or lower than that of his current lowest interest rate. How could he do that? Keep in mind that when Freddy needed dorm furniture, he only needed $1,500. When Freddy was car-shopping, he needed $20,000. When he furnished his new house, he needed $5,000. When Freddy went backpacking, he needed $8,000. He also built up a $4,000 credit card balance one little purchase at a time.

So as Freddy shows up to the bank, he isn't asking for more money. Let's be perfectly clear about that. Freddy admits to the banking partner that he's made some ill-advised decisions. But with a new understanding of how to manage his finances, he has a plan to retire this debt and is seeking help to accomplish his focused goal. He's been able to afford the payments consistently for as long as they've existed, although occasionally he has needed to wait for payday to arrive. But the debt never seems to go down.

Freddy's request is for the bank to provide him with a single loan source, in the total amount of all his outstanding balances, to eliminate the multitude of small payments he's currently making. This way, he can focus on the solution. By channelling all the debt into one place, his monthly payment will have a greater impact. He'll pay less interest, which should give him a small reprieve on his cashflow position.

As you can see, this is analogous to dropping honey to attract the ants to one place.

As the bank assesses Freddy's situation, they recognize the challenge of managing the various payments, with some interest charges as high as 19.99 percent. They know very well how long it would take to retire all these small debts individually.

So they make Freddy a new proposal, which provides him with a single loan value of $38,500. This will completely eliminate all five of his previous loans.

Based on economies of scale, which loan would have a lower interest rate—a loan for $4,000 or a loan worth ten times that much? That's right. When the bank offers you $40,000, they are generally able to do that at a lower interest rate.

As Freddy walks out of the bank, his new consolidation loan activated, he knows that he has only one area of infestation to attack. He can now direct all his troops in a focused fashion. In addition to having gained the ability to focus their attention, his overall cost of borrowing has also declined significantly. Freddy's previous interest rates averaged twelve percent, but it's now been cut to 6.25 percent, cut nearly in half. He was previously paying $1,100 per month in minimum monthly payments, and today his new monthly payment, inclusive of both principal and interest, is just $700.

Freddy has reduced the overall cost of his debt by way of reducing the interest charges he was previously exposed to, lowering his payment by a third.

At the same time, he's directing more of this monthly payment toward the principal of the loan, reducing the duration of the loan from decades to just years.

If Freddy had been having a hard time breathing under the weight of all that debt, doesn't it stand to reason that he would be able to breathe a little lighter now? Of course it does.

Strategy #2: Top-Up. For as long as Freddy can remember, he's been making those painful $1,100 debt service payments. Now he makes just one $700 payment. This means he's saving $400 per month. The next rapid debt-crunching strategy is to take half of that amount, which would be $200, and apply it directly to the principal-only portion of the new loan. This doesn't actually cost Freddy anything, because it was money he was previously paying to his lenders anyhow.

These extra "top-up" payments can reduce the life of his new consolidation loan by more than fifteen months, positioning him to be out of his bad debt position in approximately forty-five months. And if he wants to really crush it, he could apply the full $400 every month to the principal. Sure, that might be painful in the short-term, but a little pain never killed anyone. By doing this, he could destroy his debt in a little more than half the amount of time.

Isn't it amazing how much more effective a small army can be when its efforts are channelled towards a common goal? It is my opinion that the smaller your army, the bigger your effort has to be in channelling them. In other words, if you don't have a lot, you need to be very intentional with what you have.

Don't let lenders, banks, employers, or anyone else dictate to you how to deploy your troops. Be a good general and lead your soldiers in a focused effort to conquer every financial challenge you're blessed with.

Yes, you read that right: challenges are a blessing. Most people are operating under the misperception that challenges are designed to block your success, when actually they're learning opportunities. Learn something from each challenge you face, and know that if the challenge wasn't in front of you, you might reach your destination before you were ready to be there—or before it was ready for you.

> Most people are operating under the misperception that challenges are designed to block your success, when actually they're learning opportunities.

Strategy #3: Target High Interest. When starting out, you quickly realize that different loans have different interest rates associated with them. Some may be as low as zero percent, while others can be as high as twenty percent or more. So another effective strategy to reduce your debt is to attack the loan with the highest interest and work your way down to the one with the lowest. Simple, right?

A credit card with a rolling balance can expose you to extremely expensive interest rates, making it very difficult to pay it off, particularly if you're trapped in a minimum monthly payment routine. A car loan or student debt, on the other hand, may only expose you to a low interest rate—say, three or five percent.

Now, if someone came along and suggested they could get you a ten to fifteen percent return on your money immediately, wouldn't that be an investment worth considering?

If you have both a high-interest loan and a low-interest loan, delay paying back the low-interest loan as long as possible and direct as much money as you can towards your high-interest loan.

Say you have an outstanding balance on a five percent loan, and another loan at 19.99 percent. Wouldn't it be wise to use the money of the lower-interest loan to get rid of the costs associated with the higher-interest loan? How's that for simple and easy?

Directing additional funds against the highest interest rates will quickly destroy that loan. Once retired, you can then redirect your soldiers in the direction of the next highest interest balance. If you repeat this strategy, your payments become more and more effective over time. Eventually, rather than applying only $200 to your principal, you can get to $500 or $600. Your debt will shed very quickly.

But the key to being free from bad debt is to be disciplined. You must refrain from accumulating additional credit.

Taking Control

This entire process, regardless of how quickly it works, is a training exercise to help you develop into a stronger financial manager. With strength comes confidence, with confidence comes opportunity, and with opportunity comes joy. Grab hold of the above strategies and see how quickly you can take control of your army, strengthen them and the effectiveness of their assault, and begin designing the future you've always dreamed possible.

For a long time in my life, the thought of owing someone money was so crushing that it robbed me of the joy in my life. A lot of people live in that space, which is why they clump all different types of debts in the same category and fear the idea of owing anything.

In applying these strategies ourselves, Megan and I have discovered that we could enjoy far more financial joy with plenty of *good* debt in our lives than when we had even a small amount of *bad* debt. The conclusion here is that debt is not the enemy, as much as it's perceived to be. The real enemy is bad debt and the ways in which we mismanage it.

So don't be discouraged if at first it feels like you're not making much of a dent. The length of time it takes to retire your entire debt load will depend on the severity of your position and the mindset you've developed.

Once you learn how to direct your funds most effectively, you'll find yourself getting a better night's sleep. That's joyful finances in the development stage.

Mortgage Strategies

We live in a society of consumers and most people in North America will have a mortgage to manage at some point in their lives, yet little is ever taught in school about how to effectively get rid of one. It troubles me that every young person isn't taught simple debt-reductions strategies as a prerequisite for graduation.

My favourite book with respect to debt management, by far, is *Rapid Debt Reduction Strategies*, by John Avanzini and Patrick Ondrey. This book has been in print for more than thirty years, and despite its age, the principles and strategies within it are timeless. John and Patrick include amortization tables that clearly illustrate how effective each of their strategies is, directly related to the amount of dollars each can save you. I can say without any reservation that this book inspired many of my own efforts and helped me save thousands upon thousands of dollars in financing or unnecessary interest charges.

First-day payment. Among these strategies, there is one related to mortgages that Megan and I have used several times throughout the years. It's applicable to homeowners at every stage, whether you're a first-time buyer, purchasing your tenth home, or perhaps just refinancing to complete an addition on your existing home.

The strategy is known as "first-day payment." I love how simple it is. It's truly a game-changer, and it requires nothing more than making your first mortgage payment on the very same day you obtain your new loan. That's it. Done.

By making your first mortgage payment on the day the interest begins to accumulate, rather than some thirty days later when your first payment comes due, you can drastically reduce the amount of interest you pay on your mortgage. That one payment can eliminate several months, and even years, off the life of your mortgage.

Does this seem too good to be true?

You might be thinking, *This won't work for me, because my mortgage isn't new.* Rest assured that this strategy will work for anyone—not to the same extent of knocking off years of payments, but it can still hugely reduce your interest costs.

So how does it work? The savings you'll experience will be relative to three specific details related to your mortgage:

1. The length of time remaining on your mortgage term (the longer the term, the more time you will eliminate).
2. The interest rate you're paying (a higher rate means higher savings).
3. The size of your first-day payment (the bigger the payment, the bigger the savings).

Perhaps the one thing I love most about dealing with finances in general is that the results are measurable. We can actually see what works and what doesn't.

With that said, let's look at the amortization chart of a $100,000 mortgage, to be paid back over thirty years, with a five percent annual interest rate. Your monthly payment, including principal and interest, would be $533.70.

Now, when dealing with conventional mortgages, be aware that the interest is front-loaded. This means that at the beginning of your mortgage, your payment includes much more interest than it does toward the end of your mortgage life. At the beginning, you have a loan value of $100,000, and each time you make a payment that balance is slightly reduced.

In our example, that first payment of $533.70 includes $412.39 of interest while just $121.31 is applied to your principal balance.

For simplicity, we'll suggest that the loan was issued on January 1.

"Congratulations," the lender will say to you when you sign the paperwork in December. "The money will be in your account on January 1, but don't worry about a thing. Your first payment isn't due until January 31. Now, go enjoy the holidays knowing you don't have to make a payment until the end of January."

The thing the lender has forgotten to mention is that the interest will begin accumulating on January 1. Why don't they share that? For one thing, perhaps it would be a little more difficult for you to enjoy your holidays if you thought about the accumulating interest. They also know that they'll be making $412.39 that first month. They really aren't in a hurry to have you start knocking it down.

However, if you decided to make your first $533.70 payment on January 1, watch what happens:

PYMT	PYMT AMT	INTEREST	PRINCIPAL	OUSTANDING BALANCE	TOTAL INTEREST
1	$533.70	$412.39	$121.31	$99,878.69	$412.39
2	$533.70	$411.89	$121.81	$99,756.88	$824.28
3	$533.70	$411.39	$122.31	$99,634.57	$1,235.67
4	$533.70	$410.88	$122.82	$99,511.76	$1,646.55
5	$533.70	$410.38	$123.32	$99,388.43	$2,056.93
6	$533.70	$409.87	$123.83	$99,264.60	$2,466.80

By making a payment on the day the loan is initiated, the outstanding balance immediately drops by $533.70—the whole amount comes off the principal. From the chart, we can see that it would otherwise take five and a half months to reduce your balance that much through regularly scheduled payments. Furthermore, during those five and a half months, you would have paid more than $2,100 in interest. Additionally, once you make your first regular payment, the amount that goes towards the principal balance is higher than it would have been if you hadn't made that first-day payment. The net result could be a reduction of twelve months off the original amortization of your mortgage. Where else could you get a four hundred percent return on your money?

Now ask yourself this: why aren't we taught this in school, and why doesn't the bank explain it to us? Does the person selling you the mortgage even realize the power of a first-day payment?

What if you made two payments the day the loan was started? It might sound crazy, but there are a lot of situations where more money is financed than is actually needed. In the event that you borrowed $100,000 but really only needed $98,900, would you ever think to apply the additional $1,100 directly toward the principal balance right from the start?

Let's see what would happen if you did.

PYMT	PYMT AMT	INTEREST	PRINCIPAL	OUSTANDING BALANCE	TOTAL INTEREST
6	$533.70	$409.87	$123.83	$99,264.60	$2,466.80
7	$533.70	$409.36	$124.34	$99,140.26	$2876.16
8	$533.70	$408.85	$124.85	$99,015.41	$3,285.01
9	$533.70	$408.33	$125.37	$98,890.04	$3,693.34

By applying the $1,100 surplus of funds to your new loan on day one, you would eliminate nine full months of payments and save $3,693.34 in interest. That's a three hundred percent return on your money. Not bad, right?

Once again, when your first regularly scheduled payment is made on January 31, more than $4 more will be applied to the principal balance every month, smashing years off the original length of the mortgage. You're on fire!

A generous gift. Many people I know have been given gifts of large sums of money. These gifts often surround some of life's most unforgettable moments, such as getting married or buying a house for the first time. If you happen to be the recipient of such a gift at some point, wonder no longer about how to make the most of it.

Now let's see what would happen if someone gave you $5,000, and you applied it against your mortgage on the first day.

PYMT	PYMT AMT	INTEREST	PRINCIPAL	OUSTANDING BALANCE	TOTAL INTEREST
10	$533.70	$407.81	$125.89	$98,764.15	$4,101.15
11	$533.70	$407.30	$126.40	$98,637.75	$4,508.45
12	$533.70	$406.77	$126.93	$98,510.82	$4,915.22

Payment 13-35 omitted to save space

PYMT	PYMT AMT	INTEREST	PRINCIPAL	OUSTANDING BALANCE	TOTAL INTEREST
36	$533.70	$393.60	$140.10	$95,302.48	$14,515.68
37	$533.70	$393.02	$140.68	$95,161.80	$14,908.70
38	$533.70	$392.44	$141.26	$95,020.54	$15,301.14

At the start of the Bible, after God had created man and woman, He then blessed them and said, *"Be fruitful and multiply"* (Genesis 1:28, NLT). I'm not sure He had mortgages in mind when He whispered those words over Adam and Eve, but there are many examples throughout the Bible where Jesus took what was available and multiplied it many times over.

This first-day payment strategy will do exactly that. We can see that the $5,000 gift could be turned into a $15,000 windfall if applied directly to one's mortgage on the day it's initiated. That one large payment alone knocks more than three years off the front end of your mortgage, and an additional two years off the total life of your loan.

Remember that these figures are merely for illustration purposes and will vary based on the parameters of your specific loan. But the principle remains the same. The timing of that first payment is critical, and regardless of how much money you have to put down on day one, you'd be well-advised to put it all down. You've worked hard to train your soldiers. Do what you can to protect them as much as possible, whenever possible.

Now for a word of caution: many bankers would argue that if you have the extra money on hand to make a first-day payment, you'd be better off just borrowing less. For example, if you're purchasing a $100,000 home and someone decides to give you $5,000 beforehand, they may suggest that you add the $5,000 to your down-payment and lower your mortgage and its starting balance to $95,000.

To the untrained borrower, this seems sensible. After all, a $95,000 mortgage would offer you a lower monthly payment than a $100,000 mortgage, right? But how much less?

Let's compare. The regular monthly payment on a $100,000 mortgage at today's interest rates of approximately four percent would be $475.52, while that of a $95,000 mortgage with the same terms would be $451.75. So if the additional $5,000 were added to the down-payment and only $95,000 were borrowed, the monthly difference would be less than $25. It would still require thirty years to retire the mortgage, but you would pay $7,362 less in interest over that time.

In the event that you borrowed $100,000 and applied $5,000 on day one, you would eliminate a total of thirty-four payments, knocking nearly three years off the front end of the mortgage term. During that time, you would have saved $11,285 in interest. Each subsequent payment would then have an additional $17 applied to the principal balance, saving an additional $4,763 over the remaining term of the loan. Also, the mortgage would be retired twenty-two months earlier on the back end.

So the total benefit of this first-day payment would result in retiring the debt nearly five years earlier than if you'd added the $5,000 to the down-payment. You would also save nearly $16,000 in interest payments during the life of the loan.

Can you see how different the outcome is when the money is applied one way rather than the other?

Accelerated Assault

This chapter was designed to entice you to think about debt in a different way. While all debts are certainly not created equal, some debts are actually beneficial and can hang around without causing damage or provoking anxiety. Others, on the other hand, need to be eliminated without delay. Once you determine which is which, I hope you can implement some of the above ideas, or variations of them and shape them to your personal situation.

I've personally used every one of the strategies discussed in this chapter, and I've implemented several of them simultaneously. I used to await my monthly statements with anticipation—the same statements most people dread—to get excited over how much money I'd saved.

I didn't realize it at the time, but this was probably my earliest exposure to the whole concept of joyful finances. While my friends were getting more and more frustrated with their increasing debt, managing to get by on relatively small salaries, I watched my debt load steadily reduce while earning even less money than they did.

The power of multiplication is fascinating, and it can have an amazing impact on your life if you put it to work. Start at the top, develop your strategy, deploy your soldiers, and celebrate as you victoriously conquer the battlefield of debt. Charge!

15

This is my command—be strong and courageous! Do not be afraid
or discouraged. For the Lord your God
is with you wherever you go.
(Joshua 1:9, NLT)

You've read a lot to this point. Perhaps some of the topics discussed in this book have served as a reminder of things you were taught but have since forgotten, while other concepts have been fresh and exciting and you can't wait to see how they work for you.

People often read books, listen to speakers, and return from seminars excited—only to find themselves so overwhelmed with information that they're paralyzed by it all. Their dominant thought becomes, "Where do I start?" And after a month or so, their enthusiasm starts to wear down. Since no action ever gets taken, nothing changes in their lives, and consequently they fall back into the very routines that caused their initial dissatisfaction in the first place.

A year later, they may reflect on their current circumstances and once again feel a sense of disappointment, frustration, or even fear.

Perhaps I should read a book, they think to themselves. *Or go to a seminar or relisten to that podcast...*

The hope this time is that the information will motivate you to take the necessary action to bring about change.

As we approach the end of this book, however, I'm very excited to share one final strategic recommendation. This strategy has as much firepower as any of the tools we've added to your arsenal so far.

When speaking to people in their twenties, thirties, and even forties, it's common for them to say they're still waiting to start their investment journey.

"I'm waiting until my schooling is paid off…"

"I'm waiting until my car is paid off…"

"I'm waiting until I've paid off my mortgage…"

You get the picture, right? Have you ever used any of those lines, or something similar to them? I know I have, and it amazes me how often I now hear friends say the very same things.

The reason I get so excited about the next topic is that it's such a game-changer. You're about to learn of a near-magical way to reduce your personal tax expenses and develop a financial investment portfolio for you and your family.

The wait is over. You're about to implement defence (reducing expenses) and offence (increasing your income) simultaneously. Even if you have a car payment, you can implement this right now. Even if you have a mortgage balance, you can implement this right now. Even if your kids plan on going to postsecondary school one day, you can implement this right now.

And if you do, you'll be amazed at the impact it will have on your long-term financial success, and your joyful financial future!

On more occasions than I can count, I've heard it said, "Well, that won't work here. You don't know what it's like where we're from." It really is sad that people default to such positions, suggesting that their circumstances are so unique that while recommended solutions may work for someone else, nope, they just won't work for them.

I don't believe it, not for a second. But if they do believe it, they will inevitably prove themselves right.

I personally think the recommended solutions in these pages will work just fine, either exactly as described or with some modifications as they apply to a person's specific circumstances.

When I hear this kind of scepticism, what the person is saying to me is, "*I'm* not going to work for that solution," not "That *solution* won't work for me."

Sadly, this reminds me of the mail carrier who approaches a farmer sitting on his porch, only to find his dog laying in the corner groaning. When the carrier asks the farmer if the dog is okay, the farmer tells the man that the dog is laying on a tack.

"Why doesn't he move then?" asks the carrier.

"Oh, because it hurts enough for him to groan about it, but not enough for him to get up and do something about it."

Gosh, there are a lot of dogs in the world. I encourage you now: be sure that you are never that dog. If the circumstances surrounding you are anything less than favourable, do something about it. You can conquer anything you put your mind to.

Now, if you happen to live in this beautiful country of Canada with me, undoubtedly you've looked across the southern border of our country to our friends in the U.S. and at some point thought, *Boy, it must be nice to have all the financial opportunities they have over there.*[18]

As an investor, one of my top ten reasons for enjoying real estate so much is because of the tax advantages—and there is one very significant difference regarding mortgage interest tax-deductibility between Canada and the United States. In Canada, the interest on your primary mortgage is not tax-deductible. In the U.S., it is.

Is that a big deal? It sure is. When we discussed the concept of the first-day payment strategy, we illustrated how paying a little extra money upfront can have a tremendous impact on how quickly you pay down your mortgage. Can you imagine how much more quickly that mortgage would be retired if you had a couple grand of tax savings to apply each year?

Of course, most of our American friends fail to do any better than Canadians when it comes to financial management, despite this obvious advantage. Why? Because without an understanding of the benefit offered by this extra tax deductibility, it is common to direct these funds to far less significant or beneficial expenditures.

Around the time of my first mortgage in 2002, my financial education really began. They say there's no better teacher than experience, and I agree wholeheartedly. You can read this book seven times over, but until you start putting these strategies into practice, it will be impossible to really understand the impact they can have on the joy of your financial future.

After about a year of faithfully making my monthly mortgage payments, a document arrived in the mail called a mortgage statement. As I looked at that

---

[18] Unless, of course, you come from where I was born and raised in southern Ontario, in which case you actually might look to the north to see our American comrades. We find ourselves about a forty-five-minute drive south of the U.S. border. This has always caused a bit of confusion, because when we visit our cottage, which happens to be a three-hour drive into Michigan along Interstate 75, we say, "We're heading up north to Michigan for the weekend." Only a very small percentage of Canadians can say that.

document, the reality of how much interest I'd paid versus the principal balance became shockingly clear. I remember staring at the figures and thinking, *This can't be right.* How could my $6,000 worth of payments have only reduced my mortgage's balance by $1,200? It just didn't seem right.

"Well, that's just the way it is when you borrow money for a house," I was informed.

Most polite Canadians would typically reply, "Oh darn. Sorry I bothered you by asking." And that would be the end of it.

Thankfully, that response didn't resonate with me. Instead I went on a search for strategies to help reduce my mortgage interest or figure out how to use that expense as a form of tax deduction. Much of what has been included in this book resulted from my efforts during this period.

What I'm about to share with you has been purposely saved for last, because it may very well be the most significant strategy of all. When you understand this piece of wisdom, you may wonder, "Why don't we hear more about this? Why isn't everyone doing it?" The only conclusion I can reach is that anything that saves the consumer a lot of money—and I mean *a lot*—isn't likely to be promoted by the big businesses that stand to lose out on the profit.

Let me give you an example. For all we know, there may be a perfectly suitable replacement for petroleum gasoline. One that's in abundant supply, costs only a fraction to process, creates zero emissions, and would be better for the world at large. Perhaps there's an immediate fix for cancer that would be cost-efficient and very effective. If these things were true, do you think in a million years that big business would welcome either of those solutions with open arms? Heck no! Financial empires would crumble if billions of dollars were suddenly not being spent on gasoline and medicine. So even if these products were likely in existence, I doubt we would ever learn about them.

Making the Most of Mortgage Interest

It was very fortunate timing for me when I looked at that first mortgage statement in the winter of 2003, bewildered by the minimal impact my diligent monthly payments were having on my mortgage principal. At the time, Fraser Smith was becoming a Canadian wealth icon in the area of mortgage management. My first exposure to his work was his book, *The Smith Manoeuvre*, which had these words on the front cover: "Is your mortgage tax deductible? Not in Canada—unless you learn how to convert your mortgage interest into large, annual, legal and free tax deductions!" It almost sounded too shady to be legal.

As it turns out, the book was amazing! Simple to understand, easy to implement. Life-changing really.

Let's start out with a summary of Smith's book. The Smith Manoeuvre is a financial strategy designed to convert the non-deductible interest debt of a house mortgage to the deductible-interest debt of an investment loan, which simultaneously ensures the building of a *free and clear* investment portfolio.

But if this principle is so life-changing, then why did my trusted mortgage specialist look at me like I had two heads when I said, "I want to use the Smith Manoeuvre to deduct my mortgage interest from my income taxes"?

"You can't do that here," the specialist said. "What are you talking about? Interest on your primary mortgage is not tax-deductible in Canada. That's an American thing. Everyone knows that."

This would have been the common response from most mortgage specialists. In fact, it's been repeated back to me by nearly every Canadian mortgage holder I've spoken to in the last twenty years.

But the solution *is* out there, even though people don't speak about it and it isn't broadcast by the banks. The Smith Manoeuvre presents an effective strategy to help you reduce your mortgage interest expense by fifty percent— which means it also reduces the lender's mortgage interest income by the same amount.[19]

There are more moving parts to the complete strategy than I can summarize in just a few pages, but what you're about to read will point you in the right direction on how to get started. With this information you'll be armed with enough ammo to approach any reputable bank and introduce yourself with the confidence that you're really taking seriously this battlefield against interest and bad debt, blazing a path for the kind of joyful financial future you've always dreamed of.

If you've been working with the same banker for many years, they're likely to look at you differently when you walk through their office doors this time.

"What's gotten into you?" your banker may ask. "Are you all right?"

"I'm better than all right," you can reply. "I'm excited about my financial future. I've decided that I need to make some changes to my current financial plan, and I'm starting today. Are you interested in working with me on this?"

---

[19] Thank you, Fraser Smith, for your efforts to market the following strategy. His son Robinson Smith has now picked up the torch and carries on his father's legacy. While I'm going to summarize my interpretation of their work over the next few pages, I encourage you to visit their website, www.smithman.net, for even more information, testimonials, and reference materials that are sure to inspire you.

Once they wipe the shock off their face, you can begin explaining some of the strategies you've learned here. And when you finish off by introducing the Smith Manoeuvre, there's a very good chance that initial look of shock will return.

Prepare yourself: you may have to find another person to deal with if your current banker simply cannot grasp the reality of your new decisions. Don't be discouraged. Many people in the banking industry aren't aware of anything more than what their employer wants them to be aware of. In essence, it's their job to sell the bank's products and services, and therefore many of the tools we've discussed in this book will be foreign to them. The bank may frown on offering such solutions because it isn't necessarily in their own best interest. If that is the case, you're at the wrong bank and need to relocate your financial affairs without delay.

Strap yourself in. As you read the following pages, you're likely to find yourself tempted to jump around the room, phone your banker, and tell all your friends. But stay put. Read through to the end, perhaps come back to this point and read it again so it sinks in. Then do some additional research on the ideas presented, to eliminate the possibility that these are just my own ideas you might be buying into.

Many have done exactly what I'm about to share with you, but many more have been discouraged by the ignorance of those around them. Brace yourself for the reality that when you share the basics related to the Smith Manoeuvre, people are going to immediately get sceptical because they haven't implemented it themselves. It's always easier to say "That won't work here" or "That doesn't work for people like us" than it is to admit that they simply don't understand something.

To protect the benefit this process could have for you, be sure to understand it well before you allow others to try and deter you. This was a really important lesson for me. I had to remember that most of the people I spoke to about finances were either in the same boat as me, or in many cases even worse off than I was. None of them looked to be really joyful about their financial future. We soon decided to only take financial advice from people who were going in the same direction we wanted to go, or seemingly had already arrived there.

The Setup

Your personal financial position probably resembles something similar to what we've identified previously in this book. Perhaps you have a handful of loans with varying balances and associated interest rates. Maybe your income is dependent on your ongoing ability to wake up and perform a job for someone in exchange for a paycheque you're not entirely thrilled about, and you cling to the hope that one day, when all your debts are reduced or eliminated, you'll still have enough time to put a bunch of money in an investment that will then mysteriously turn into a mountainous pile capable of sustaining your lifestyle until your final breath.

Sounds good, right?

Except it doesn't work—because there are always new expenses, new debts, and new setbacks. And the one thing that keeps eluding you is irreplaceable, and you're running out of it more and more every day: time! We never know how much time we have left. All we can count on is that we have less of it remaining every minute that slips by.

So should you wait to start taking control of your future? It's a dangerous and risky move. This is one of those cases where no action is absolutely more risky than taking some action, and yet people state every day, "I'm going to wait until…" But what if that thing they're waiting for never comes to pass? Will they ever start? And even if they do start, will they have enough time left to accomplish anything significant? Decide today that this is the perfect time to start. Today! Right now! Put the excuses aside and study the following strategy to learn how the Smith Manoeuvre can help you start something amazing right now.

> Decide today that this is the perfect time to start. Today! Right now!

We've already established that the interest being paid on your primary mortgage isn't tax-deductible in Canada. Additional interest—such as on car loans, vacations, and pesky credit cards—isn't tax-deductible, either.

But there is a type of interest that the Canadian government does consider to be tax-deductible, and the following strategy uses this interest to reduce your taxes and increase your financial position immediately.

For our American friends reading this, please stay with us. Although you are already eligible to deduct the interest on your primary mortgage, there are elements of this strategy you can also use to fast-track your investment plan.

In Canada, when you borrow to invest—whether it be mutual funds, RRSPs, real estate, or even small business—the government allows you to use the interest related to the borrowed funds as a tax-deductible expense.

Going back to our prior discussion about assets and liabilities, most people spend their entire lives buying liabilities and thinking they're assets, only to find out in the end that they have very little actual assets because their liabilities ate up all their money.

Well, this is one of those times when the government actually gives you a bit of a heads up on whether they think your house is an asset or a liability. Because they realize that a house is a liability to the owner occupant, they don't permit you to deduct the interest on the mortgage. That should be a sign. On the other hand, if you purchased an income property, the loan on that property would include tax-deductible interest.

One is an asset, the other a liability. Does that make sense? One puts money in your pocket, or at least has the potential to, while the other simply takes money out of your pocket.

What Fraser Smith and his son Robinson have illustrated beautifully is how to borrow for investment purposes and use your available cash to pay down non-tax-deductible expenses. Straight out of the gate, you can develop an investment portfolio that uses time to its benefit, permitting compounding interest to work in your favour while generating a new source of income from the tax-deductible interest you've never had before.

To set yourself up to begin receiving refund cheques from the Canadian government, rapidly pay down your mortgage, and start building an investment portfolio, you need to arrange three simple things: an *appraisal* on your home to establish its lending value, a good *financial planner* who understands what you're trying to achieve, and a banker who will provide you with a *re-advanceable mortgage* program. Once you have these items in place, you can start right away and have the rest of your life to optimize your debt, investments, and cashflow. There's no need to wait any longer to begin.

The risks for your retirement will be rather modest if you start now to generate free money for your family via tax refund cheques from the government. The point is, you're paying a huge amount of interest as part of your mortgage payment every month. The Smith Manoeuvre allows you to change the character of that interest expense—from the bad kind to the good kind—by converting the interest expense to tax deductions.

You don't need to increase your debt to do this. This is not a leveraging strategy. It's a debt conversion strategy. And you don't need to spend more of your own money to make this happen, either, since you're already spending this money on your mortgage payment. It's a relatively simple rearrangement of your financial affairs.

Since we've already established the difference between good and bad debts, you will understand the following excerpt from a Smith Manoeuvre presentation that someone sent me in 2008:

> Any planner will tell you that reducing income tax is one of the most efficient ways that exist in order to improve your personal net worth. That's because you have to earn $1,000 in order to have $600 to spend if you are at the 40% tax bracket. The interest in the first year on your $200,000 mortgage at 7% is about $14,000, non-deductible. If you had implemented The Smith Manoeuvre, you would have a $14,000 tax deduction to claim. Furthermore, you could have this $14,000 tax deduction *every year for the rest of your life.* My objective for all Canadian mortgage holders is that they die at age 130 still owing the bank $200,000, still claiming $14,000 per year every year in tax deductions, and living off of the income of a huge portfolio of several million dollars that represents the compounding of $200,000 for all those years. What a wonderful personal pension plan. That's what wealthy people do. So can you.

How It Works

With the proper tools in place and the right team of advisors to work with, the solution is to make seventy-five percent of the equity in your home work for you *right now.* The plan includes getting rid of your bad debt mortgage, building an investment portfolio, and getting free tax refund cheques, all at the same time. It's also crucial to get professional assistance from a financial planner who has the education to build a personalized plan for you so you can optimize all the benefits of the Smith Manoeuvre.

You can attempt this on your own, but you're unlikely to have the knowledge to optimize the opportunity.

For the sake of illustration, we'll work with a scenario that includes a home with an appraised value of $200,000. If there were a mortgage in place equal to seventy-five percent of the appraised value, or twenty-five percent equity in the home, this is a great starting point. Most banks want at least twenty-five percent equity in a home, otherwise the owner only qualifies for expensive high-ratio mortgages with huge extra expense. Twenty-five percent equity gives the bank comfort and the owner a safety margin.

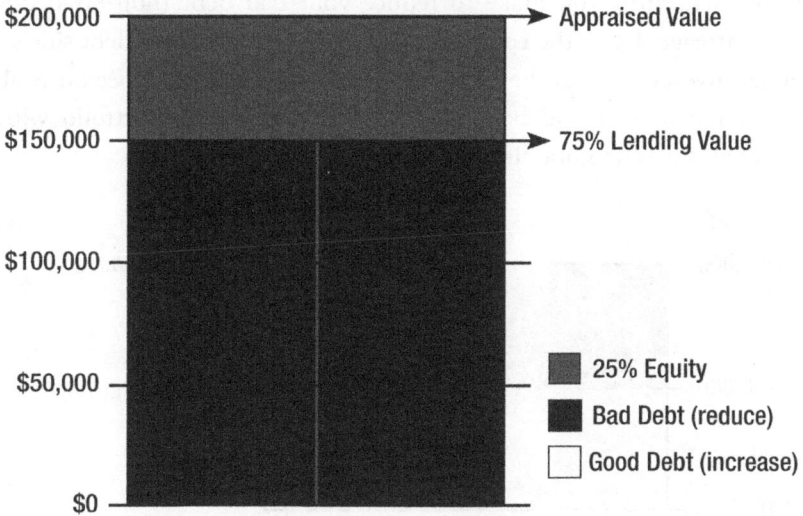

When you work with a financial planner, they'll initiate the re-advanceable mortgage product that will set you up to begin the transfer from bad debt to good debt. As the bad debt (dark) is reduced, whether because you're making regular monthly payments or occasional overpayments, the money is reborrowed (light) and invested. If the average reduction of the mortgage by regular payments for the next twelve months is, say, $500 per month, then it would seem safe to set up a $500 per month pre-authorized chequing withdrawal to purchase investments.

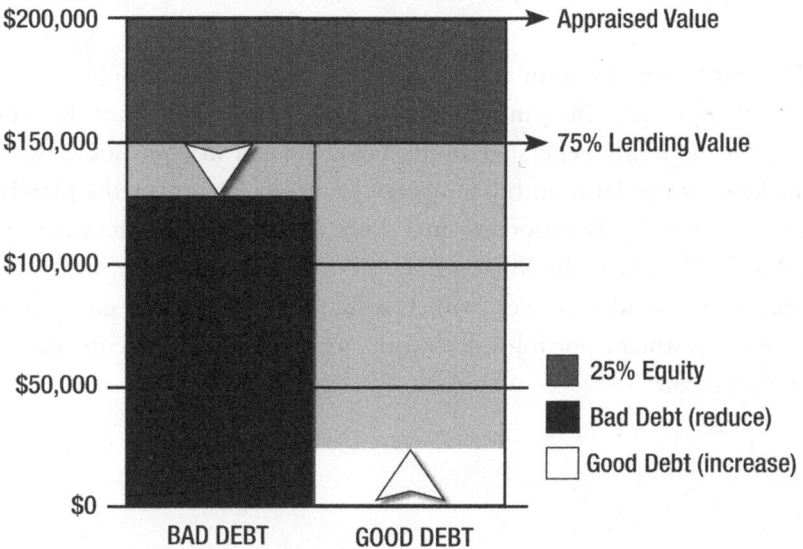

With each effort you make to reduce your bad debt (non-tax-deductible interest mortgage debt), the equity is re-advanced on the good debt side so that additional investments can be purchased. Can you see how a person is able to reduce their bad debt and begin building an investment portfolio with free money, all at the exact same time, without having to wait?

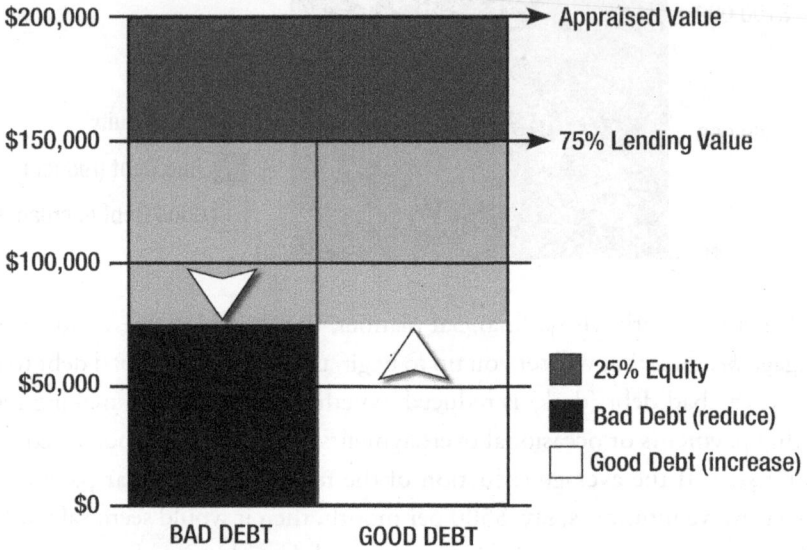

Pay particular attention to the fact that no additional debt is acquired through this process. The funds being used to purchase your new investments come from the newly generated equity being created in your home each time you make your regular monthly mortgage payment. Even once the plan is fully executed, the good debt becomes equal to the bad debt the homeowner initially started with. The two main differences in this homeowner's life, however, are that they get a tax refund every year, which is free money from the government, as well as an investment portfolio that works to generate investment income that didn't exist before.

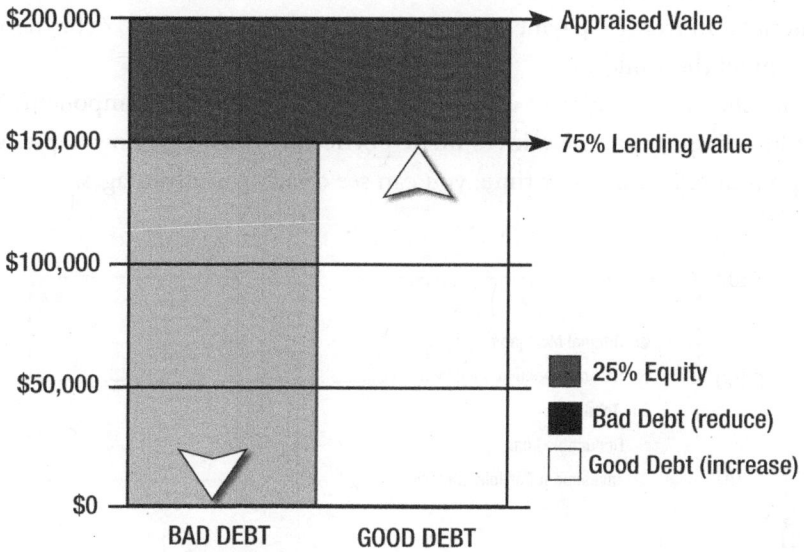

Perhaps it would be easier to look at it a different way, still recognizing the value of pictures for the use of explanation. This is what happens if you know to ask the bank to reorganize your loan structure:

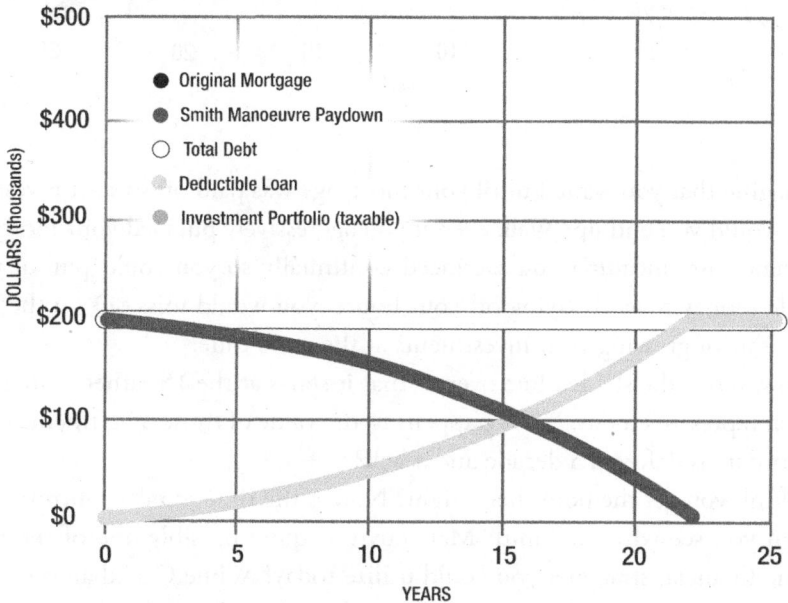

What we see here is that the deductible loan balance increased as the non-deductible mortgage payment was reduced—and the total debt remained constant all the while.

But the most significant element of all is the investment component. When we add a line for the new investment portfolio, which can now capitalize on compounding interest over time, you can see clearly the advantages:

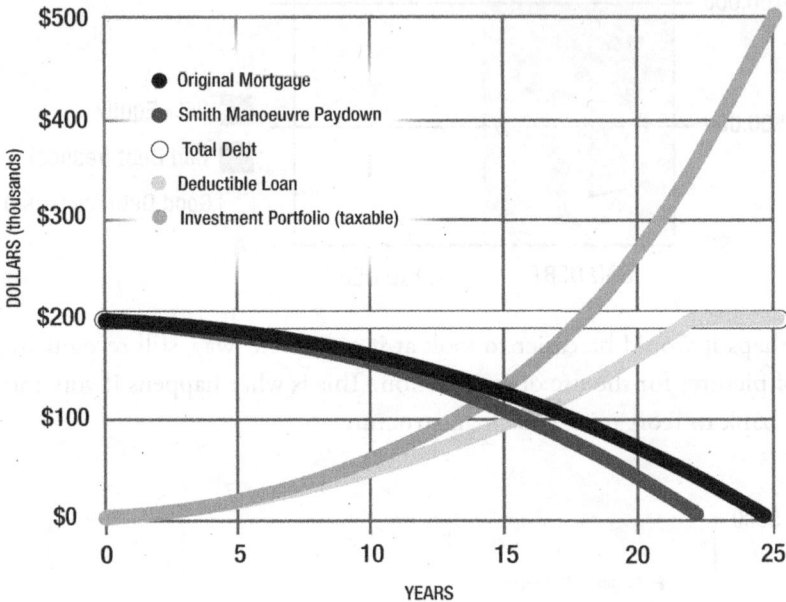

Imagine that you waited until your mortgage was paid off to start investing. Where would you end up? Well, even if you aggressively pursued your mortgage retirement date, meaning you sacrificed continually so you could put all your available money toward paying off your house, you would miss out on the next fifteen years of growing your investments at the same time.

Now, move the shaded line over so that it starts at the 15 rather than at the 0, which represents today. What happens to the value of those investments when the start date is deferred a decade and a half?

I think you get the point here, right? Now is the time to take control.

Can you see why the Smith Manoeuvre is quite possibly one of the most dynamic financial strategies you could utilize today? While Canadian mortgage holders stand to gain the most from it, because of our limiting financial restrictions, the principle remains the same whether you have a mortgage on your home or not, and whether you live in Canada or not. Every homeowner who wants to create a joyful financial future can benefit.

Four Easy Steps

Here is a breakdown of the steps involved in following the plain jane Smith Manoeuvre:

1. Reborrow and invest any paydowns on your first mortgage.
2. Apply tax refunds against your first mortgage, then immediately reborrow and invest the same amount.

And here's how you can follow the enhanced Smith Manoeuvre:

3. Cash in and apply current paid-up assets against the first mortgage in the morning, then reborrow and invest the same amount in the afternoon.
4. Divert any monthly savings or investment programs against the first mortgage, and immediately reborrow and invest the same amount.[20]

At the conclusion of his presentations, Fraser Smith would remind people that procrastination is the enemy of your financial success. So what are you waiting for? You now have an army, a loaded arsenal, and a book of strategies that can help you tackle any battlefield you want. You owe it to yourself to take the next steps today. You owe it to your family. Be the leader you were born to be, lead your troops into victory, and enjoy the joyful financial future you always dreamed of. The next move is yours!

---

[20] For more information on the Smith Manoeuvre, visit www.smithman.net, or visit us on Facebook by searching for "The Joyful Series."

Conclusion: Take Command

*Don't be afraid, for I am with you. Don't be discouraged, for I am
your God. I will strengthen you and help you. I will hold you up
with my victorious right hand.*
(Isaiah 41:10, NLT)

You have now invested significant time, in addition to the cost of this book, learning how to position yourself to design, lay out a plan, and defend and attack a joyful financial future. You deserve to celebrate that achievement, since many never even get this far.

But what will you do with the information you have now? We've discussed over and over throughout the book the fact that knowledge and personal growth are the best investments you can make, but how many people much smarter than you and me die broke? Or worse, having known nothing better than financial anxiety their entire lives? Perhaps they had the knowledge you have now, and more, and yet failed to develop a joyful financial position in life.

The answer has two sides. First, such people either lack a vision of what they could have, or they lack the belief that's required to create the necessary action. Do not allow these people to discourage you. Take the information you've learned and put it to work for you. It's all here, and the more you understand what these strategies are capable of, the more you will realize the benefit they can bring to your current and future life.

You don't have to put money in a shoebox and wait thirty or forty years to see what it's worth. You can start today and begin to see results inside of thirty days. It's that powerful! You hold in your hand the keys to unlock any doors that have been holding you back. Take command now, organize your soldiers, build your army, strategize a plan, and then take charge. Go after it! Everything you've dreamed of is waiting on the other side of action.

Fuel for the Tank

Each book in the Joyful Series begins and ends in a similar fashion, calling you to bring to mind what makes your motor crank. Undoubtedly, you realize that regardless of how valuable the car in your driveway is, it simply will not run if it doesn't have sufficient fuel. Not only is it important for that vehicle to have the proper kind of fuel, the fuel must not be stale, and there must be enough fuel in the tank for the vehicle to get from where it is to where you want it to take you.

What does the fuel in your tank look like right now? I would like to think that you have just put the proper kind of fuel in your tank, and that it is fresh and new.

Now comes the difficult part, though: is it enough? Not likely. One book simply doesn't pack enough power, in most cases, for you to ignite your vehicle and motor down the highway of life to the destination of your desires. But you can top it up right now.

To increase the volume of fuel just added to your tank, you need to be reminded of what's important to you. What do you look forward to in the future? Where do you want this vehicle to take you? How far do you want to travel, who do you want to bring with you, and what will it look like when you get there?

Perhaps you're an island beachcomber, and you get excited about those long walks along the shoreline with your feet only inches in the water as the crystal-clear waves rock gently against the sandy beach. As your toes sink into that warm, soothing mixture of grain and water, you feel the kiss of the late afternoon sunshine on your cheek. A delicate breeze blows across your shoulders, assuring you that tomorrow will be just as beautiful as today. And as you peer out at the sailor's sky, you're filled with peaceful comfort knowing that you have another day to look forward to this wonderful canvas.

Maybe you're not the beachcomber type. Perhaps home is where your heart is, and you just wish the rest of you could be there more often. Do you yearn to be a more present part of your family and home life? Can you envision a time that includes you waking up with your spouse first thing in the morning and spending quality wake-up time together? No alarm clocks, no agenda, no "Shoot, I'm late already" the moment you see the time.

Your children arise from bed to greet you with smiles and hugs that would warm the deepest of deep freezes. Can you smell those pancakes cooking in the kitchen, or that fresh cup of coffee as you sip it and look out the back window to see animals frolicking in the yard?

As your children leave for school—yeah, this kind of day can happen every day of the week now, not just on holidays or the occasional Sunday—you wink to your spouse as you retreat to your favourite place in the house or on the property. You've been working on a hobby and each day you spend time just tinkering with materials, exploring your creative side as your best-loved songs play in the background.

As the afternoon passes and the children return home, you greet them at the end of the driveway. You then return to the house for your afternoon briefing and snack time. Later, dinnertime includes interactive engagement between all members of the family as you learn about what each of your children did that day, who they played with, what they learned, what challenges they're facing, and what they look forward to most about tomorrow.

Once the kids retire for the night, you and your spouse are left with some adult conversation as you sit on the porch swing to watch the sun finally retire for the night as well. The peace and comfort that fills your every cell, from the bottom of your toes to the hair on the top of your head, has been generated by your total involvement and presence in your family. You go to bed knowing that tomorrow will be more of the same, because you understand that days like these are numbered—and thankfully, you're making the most of each one you have.

Does that top up your tank and provide you with enough fuel to sustain the effort necessary to put the things you've learned into practice?

Step one of your strategy is to build the dream that suits you. Sure, the steps outlined in this book may seem nice, for someone else—but if they aren't designed specifically for you, to make your motor crank, then taking them may not be any different than putting old fuel in your tank and expecting your vehicle to operate at high performance. Design the dream that moves you, and then read, reread, and read this book again until you memorize that dream, until you know every detail of it. At that point, you will have topped up your tank. Putting into practice what you've just learned in this book will then seem essential and urgent.

That's where the power will really begin.

What Have You Learned?

Aside from some great stories, what have you learned throughout these pages? Have you learned that God wants you to be prosperous? Throughout the first thirty years of my faith walk, I was led to believe that if you were a good Catholic or Christian, you had to be broke. If you were financially resourceful by any means, it seemed that you weren't giving enough.

Scripture is often used to support these ideas, such as Matthew 19:24, which reads, *"And again I say to you, it is easier for a camel to go through the eye of a needle than for a rich man to enter the kingdom of God"* (NKJV). Well, if you believe that, why in the world would you ever want to live in a big house or drive a nice car? It would appear that you'll be eternally damned if you do.

But that is not the case at all. In fact, further review of that scripture reveals that Jesus encourages us to obey the Ten Commandments, and in doing so we will enter the kingdom of God. However, a man who covets earthly possessions and makes those things his god is a man who will not be granted passage beyond this world. Jesus's instruction is to give the first ten percent of your harvest, thus retaining ninety percent for yourself.

The greatest support in the argument that God wants you to be prosperous comes from the fact that ten percent of a lot is much more influential and can do much more good in the world than ten percent of a little. If your heart is right and you are well-intended with your resources, you will find that God's provision will always be greater than that which you can create on your own.

Now that you know you were destined for financial prosperity, have you learned to develop a new perspective on money itself? Do you now see why it is said that the wealthy have money working for them, while the middle class spend their entire lives working for money?

We discussed the idea of treating each dollar as a soldier, committed to taking up your battle in the war against financial mediocrity. Treat these soldiers well, give them a safe home to grow, multiply them in numbers and develop them in strength, and you will soon have a powerful army of your own.

Of course, no army is powerful without a battlefield to compete on. After reading *Joyful Finances*, you have been exposed to several battlefields you can opt to conquer. Selecting one that suits your interest, studying the ins and outs of that battlefield, and putting a strategy in place that will increase your odds of success is all part of the journey you've just completed.

There are likely to be pitfalls and snares down any path you choose to walk, so travel carefully as you advance into unfamiliar territories. Lean on others who have already conquered that battlefield, remaining cautiously sceptical so as to protect yourself from those who have failed before you. One person's failure certainly does not represent an impossible to beat challenge, so stay alert and learn from another's failure just as you do their victories.

Keep your dreams in front of you the entire time. If at some point you feel like you're losing steam—it may be that you feel defeated because you suffered a loss or setback to your plan—review your dream again. Pull out the roadmap and look at your final destination, keeping in mind that success is a journey, inclusive of all the ups and downs that it is sure to include. No successful person ever went from beginning to end without some trials and tribulations. The prize doesn't go to the man who never falls; the prize goes to the man who continues to get up after every fall. You will fall. That's okay. Just get back up and keep going. Victory is yours to be taken.

Well, that's it. You've got it—a motive, a strategy, an understanding of the battlefield landscape. The only thing missing is your army. Go now and begin building yours. Take control of your financial destiny in a way you never before thought possible. You have all the tools to eliminate the financial strife and anxiety in your life.

By this time next year, you may not be cruising the seven seas in your sailboat, but I can assure you that with discipline and patience, you can turn your circumstances around so that joyful finances are part of·your everyday life from this day forward.

The next move is yours, General. Now go take action!

About the Author

Beginning at a young age of ten, Ryan began recognizing financial opportunities where most people could not. Turning trash to cash was his first exposure to passive income, and it directed him on a path that would find him challenging nearly every financial principle his family had raised him in.

Born into a loving Catholic family from southwestern Ontario, Canada, Ryan grew up in a community driven by the automotive industry. His home was on the opposite side of the Detroit River, across from Detroit, Michigan—Motor City. Blue collar families kept the industry in motion, and these middle-class people were continuously affected by the performance of each vehicle introduced to the market. His family's discussions around the dinner table included shift work, two-week summer holidays, commuter vans, and overtime opportunities.

Nearly thirty years into his career, when faced with extreme adversity, Ryan recognized the voice of God calling him to turn the wheel and head in a new direction.

With the spirit of an entrepreneur, Ryan realized early that there had to be other ways to meet his financial goals than committing to the life of a factory worker. Although it was an unpopular decision at the time, he decided to end his post-secondary education after completing just one year, accepting an entry-level job to earn enough money to survive. But most importantly, Ryan began to blaze his own path to financial prosperity.

In *Joyful Finances*, Ryan shares significant insights on how to turn a gloomy financial forecast into something you can get excited about and look forward to.